CW01474851

Brilliant Business Entrepreneurship

Niall McCreanor, M.B.S

For Jacinta, Oisín, Erin and Faolán

My World!

Contents

i.   Introduction to Entrepreneurship

Shane and Venkataraman (2000) say that entrepreneurship is a complicated and multifaceted idea that has been looked at from many different fields of study. Aldrich and Fiol (1994) say that entrepreneurship is all about starting and running new businesses with the goal of making money for everyone involved.

Over time, scholars and business owners have given different definitions and points of view on what it means to be an entrepreneur. Schumpeter wrote in 1934 that entrepreneurs were the ones who caused creative destruction by bringing new products, services, and technologies to the market. Kirzner (1973), on the other hand, focused on the role of entrepreneurs in finding and taking advantage of market inefficiencies. Stevenson and Gumpert (1985) highlighted the importance of entrepreneurial teams in building successful businesses.

In recent years, entrepreneurship has gotten a lot of attention because it has the potential to boost economic growth, create jobs, and encourage innovation (Braunerhjelm & Acs, 2015). Small businesses, for example, which are defined as firms with fewer than 500 employees, account for almost half of the private sector workforce and 99.9% of all firms in the United States (U.S. Small Business Administration, 2022). Because entrepreneurship can help the economy grow, policymakers, academics, and the general public are becoming more and more interested in it.

Definition of entrepreneurship

Entrepreneurship is the process of finding and pursuing opportunities to create new and valuable products, services, or business models that meet unmet needs or solve existing problems in a way that is sustainable and profitable. It means taking calculated risks, gathering resources, and building networks to turn ideas into reality and create value for customers, employees, investors, and society as a whole. Entrepreneurship requires a mix of vision, creativity, leadership, persistence, and the ability to change with the times and learn from mistakes.

The importance of entrepreneurship

Shane (2018) says that entrepreneurship is a key driver of economic growth, job creation, and innovation. (Braunerhjelm & Acs, 2015) Entrepreneurs help find new business opportunities and bring new products, services, and business models to the market.

According to a report by the Global Entrepreneurship Monitor, there were approximately 582 million entrepreneurs worldwide in 2020, and around 63 million new businesses were started that year alone (Amorós et al., 2021). (Acs & Stough, 2015) These entrepreneurs not only make jobs, but they also help local economies grow by making new money and opening up new markets.

Entrepreneurs not only help the economy, but they are also very important for driving innovation and societal growth (Baumol, 2010). Entrepreneurs challenge the status quo with their creative and disruptive ideas. They break down barriers to entry and find solutions to hard problems (Schumpeter, 1934).

Entrepreneurship is also linked to other good things, like personal and professional growth (Chandler and Lyon, 2001). Starting and running a business can provide entrepreneurs with opportunities for personal growth, such as developing new skills, building confidence, and learning from failures.

Governments and policymakers around the world have recognised the importance of entrepreneurship and implemented policies and programmes to support its development (Braunerhjelm & Acs, 2015). These policies include funding for research and development, tax incentives for small businesses, and training and education programmes for entrepreneurs (Acs & Szerb, 2017).

Entrepreneurship is crucial for economic growth, job creation, and innovation. Entrepreneurs are the driving force behind new ventures and bring new products, services, and business models to the market. They also play a critical role in driving societal development and personal and professional growth. As such, it is important for governments and policymakers to support entrepreneurship development and create an environment that fosters entrepreneurial activity.

The benefits of becoming an entrepreneur

People who are willing to take the risk of starting and running their own businesses can get a lot of personal and professional benefits from doing so (Baumol, 2010). Some of the most significant benefits of becoming an entrepreneur include:

> ➤ Pursuing passion and creativity

Entrepreneurship provides an opportunity to pursue one's passion and creativity by building a business around a product or service that one truly cares about (Shane, 2018). Entrepreneurs often start businesses in areas that they are passionate about, which can lead to a greater sense of fulfilment and purpose in their work.

> ➤ Control over work and personal life

Entrepreneurs have greater control over their work and personal lives, as they are able to set their own schedules and work on projects that they find meaningful (Baumol, 2010). This can lead to a better work-life balance and a greater sense of autonomy.

> ➤ Potential for Financial Rewards

Entrepreneurship can also provide the potential for significant financial rewards. Successful entrepreneurs can build valuable businesses that generate significant profits, leading to greater financial security and wealth (Shane, 2018).

> Personal and professional growth

Starting and running a business requires a range of skills, including leadership, problem-solving, and communication, among others (Chandler & Lyon, 2001). Entrepreneurs are always being asked to improve these skills, which can help them grow both personally and professionally.

> Positive Impact on Society

(Braunerhjelm & Acs, 2015) Entrepreneurship has the potential to do good things for society by creating jobs, introducing new products and services, and helping the economy grow. Entrepreneurs who are successful can start businesses that not only make money but also help society in important ways.

Entrepreneurship can be difficult and requires a lot of hard work and dedication, but it has a lot of benefits. For those with a passion for innovation and a willingness to take risks, entrepreneurship can provide a path to personal and professional fulfilment, financial success, and a positive impact on society.

Common misconceptions about entrepreneurship

People often think of entrepreneurship as a fun and profitable way to make a living, but there are a few common misconceptions that can stop people from pursuing it. These misconceptions can prevent potential entrepreneurs from taking the leap, even if they have a great idea and the drive to succeed. Here are some of the most common myths about starting a business, along with real-world examples that show how wrong they are:

➢ Entrepreneurs are born, not made.

One of the most common myths about entrepreneurship is that successful entrepreneurs are born with traits like creativity, taking risks, and coming up with new ideas. However, research has shown that while some traits, such as passion and persistence, may be helpful for entrepreneurs, they alone are not sufficient for success (Cardon et al., 2009). Entrepreneurship is a learned skill that can be developed through education, training, and experience.

Real-world example: Sara Blakely, the founder of Spanx, did not have a background in fashion or business when she started her company. Instead, she came up with the idea for Spanx while working as a salesperson and trying to find a solution to the problem of visible panty lines. Despite not having a background in the industry, she taught herself about fabrics, manufacturing, and retail and built a billion-dollar company from scratch.

> ➢ Entrepreneurship is only for the young.

Another misconception about entrepreneurship is that it is only for the young. While it is true that many successful entrepreneurs start their businesses at a young age, there is no age limit for entrepreneurship (Bhide, 1992). In fact, many entrepreneurs start their businesses later in life, after gaining experience and expertise in their chosen fields.

Real-world example: Harland Sanders, the founder of KFC, did not start his franchise until he was in his sixties. Before that, he had worked in a variety of jobs, including steamboat pilot, insurance salesman, and gas station owner. He only started cooking and selling fried chicken after his retirement, but his recipe and business model proved so successful that KFC became a global fast-food giant.

> ➢ Entrepreneurship requires a large amount of capital.

Many people assume that starting a business requires a large amount of capital and that without significant financial resources, entrepreneurship is not possible. However, while access to capital can be important for starting and growing a business, there are many other factors that can impact an entrepreneur's chances of success, such as market demand, competition, and the regulatory environment (Aldrich & Fiol, 1994).

Real-world illustration: The co-founders of Apple, Steve Jobs and Steve Wozniak, started their company with just $1,300, which they raised by selling a van and a calculator. They used this money to build the first Apple computer in Jobs' garage, and over time, the company grew into one of the most valuable in the world.

> Entrepreneurship is a solo endeavour.

Some people think that being an entrepreneur is a solo job and that to be successful, an entrepreneur must work alone. However, successful entrepreneurs often work with teams of individuals who share their vision and can help them achieve their goals (Stevenson & Gumpert, 1985).

Real-world example: Elon Musk, the founder of Tesla and SpaceX, is known for his ambitious and innovative ideas. However, he has also surrounded himself with talented teams of engineers, designers, and businesspeople who help him turn his ideas into reality. Without the support of his teams, Musk would not have been able to achieve his many successes.

Some common myths about entrepreneurship can stop people from pursuing it as a career. However, these myths are not always true, and people from all walks of life and experiences can pursue entrepreneurship and be successful at it. By spotting and busting these myths, people who want to start their own businesses can gain the confidence they need to follow their dreams and build successful businesses.

ii.   Theories of Entrepreneurship

Scholars from many different fields have done a lot of research on entrepreneurship, which has led to the creation of many theories and frameworks that try to explain what entrepreneurs do (Shane & Venkataraman, 2000). Theories of entrepreneurship help us understand what makes people want to start and grow businesses, what problems they face, and what results they get.

Entrepreneurship theories can be put into several broad groups, such as individual-level theories, theories that focus on opportunities, theories that focus on resources, and theories that focus on networks, among others (Chandler & Hanks, 1994). Each type of theory has a different way of looking at entrepreneurship, focusing on different parts of the process and the things that affect it.

In this chapter, we'll look at some of the most important theories of entrepreneurship. We'll talk about their main ideas, assumptions, and what they mean for business. By understanding these theories, people who want to be entrepreneurs can learn more about how businesses work and what makes them successful. People who are already running businesses can use these insights to come up with better ways to build and grow their businesses.

Economic and sociological theories of entrepreneurship

Entrepreneurship has been looked at from many different angles, like economics and sociology. Each of these fields has come up with a different set of theories to explain what entrepreneurs do.

Economic Theories of Entrepreneurship

Economic theories of entrepreneurship focus on the factors that drive individuals to start businesses and the economic outcomes of their actions (Baumol, 1990). The opportunity-cost theory is one of the most influential economic theories of entrepreneurship. It says that people are motivated to start their own businesses when the potential returns from starting a business are higher than the returns they could earn in their current job (Knight, 1921). This theory suggests that entrepreneurship is a rational decision that is based on the expected returns from investing time, money, and other resources in a new venture. For example, a person who has a job but wants to start a business might weigh the potential financial rewards of entrepreneurship against the security and stability of their current job.

The resource-based view is another economic theory of entrepreneurship. It emphasises how important resources and skills are in determining how well an entrepreneur does (Barney, 1991). This theory suggests that entrepreneurs who have access to valuable resources, such as financial capital, human capital, or social capital, are more likely to succeed than those who do not. For example, an entrepreneur with a strong network of business contacts might be better able to get funding, attract customers, and form partnerships than one who doesn't.

The transaction cost theory is another economic theory of entrepreneurship that suggests that entrepreneurship can emerge as a response to market imperfections and transaction costs (Williamson, 1985). This theory suggests that entrepreneurs can create value by reducing transaction costs, such as search costs, bargaining costs, and coordination costs. For example, an entrepreneur who develops an online platform that connects buyers and sellers in a niche market can reduce the transaction costs associated with finding and negotiating with potential business partners.

Examples of Economic Theories of Entrepreneurship:

> ➢ **Opportunity-cost theory:** A person who has a job as an accountant but wants to start a marketing agency may weigh the potential financial rewards of entrepreneurship against the security and stability of their current job.
> ➢ **Resource-based view:** An entrepreneur with a strong network of business contacts may be better able to get funding, attract customers, and form partnerships than one who doesn't.
> ➢ **Transaction cost theory** says that an entrepreneur who creates an online platform that connects buyers and sellers in a niche market can lower the costs of finding and negotiating with potential business partners.

Sociological Theories of Entrepreneurship

Sociological theories of entrepreneurship, on the other hand, focus on the social and cultural factors that influence entrepreneurial behaviour and outcomes (Aldrich & Martinez, 2001). The institutional theory is an important sociological theory of entrepreneurship. It says that entrepreneurs are shaped by the norms, values, and practises of the larger social and institutional environment in which they work (DiMaggio and Powell, 1983). This theory says that entrepreneurs have to find their way through a complicated network of social, political, and economic institutions that can help or hurt their success. For instance, entrepreneurs who work in industries with a lot of rules may face more problems than those who work in industries with fewer rules.

The network theory is another sociological theory of entrepreneurship. It focuses on how social networks give entrepreneurs access to resources, information, and support (Granovetter, 1985). This theory suggests that entrepreneurs who have strong social networks are more likely to be successful than those who do not. For example, an entrepreneur who is well connected to other entrepreneurs, investors, and industry experts may be able to tap into their knowledge, expertise, and resources to build a successful business.

Examples of sociological theories of entrepreneurship:

> ➤ **Institutional theory** says that entrepreneurs who work in industries with a lot of rules may have more problems than those who work in industries with less rules.
> ➤ **Network theory:** An entrepreneur who is well connected to other entrepreneurs, investors, and industry experts may be able to tap into their knowledge, expertise, and resources to build a successful business.

Theories of entrepreneurship from the fields of economics and sociology can help us understand how complex and changing entrepreneurship is. By understanding these theories and putting them to use in the real world, entrepreneurs can learn more about what makes them successful, and policymakers can use this information to come up with better ways to encourage entrepreneurship and economic growth.

The role of innovation and creativity

Innovation and creativity are important parts of entrepreneurship because they are often the main reasons why a business succeeds (Shane, 2000). Entrepreneurs need to be innovative and creative to find and take advantage of new opportunities, set themselves apart from competitors, and give their customers something of value.

Schumpeter's (1934) theory of "creative destruction" is an important way to understand the role of innovation in business. This theory says that entrepreneurs make the economy grow by making new products, services, and processes that shake up markets and industries that are already there. For example, Airbnb changed the hotel business by giving people a new way to rent out their homes or apartments to travellers. This put pressure on the traditional hotel business. In a similar way, Tesla changed the auto industry by making electric cars that are better in terms of performance, design, and the environment than traditional gas-powered cars.

Entrepreneurs also need to be creative because they need to be able to come up with new ideas and ways to solve problems (Amabile, 1996). Sarasvathy's (2001) effectuation theory is a framework that talks about how important creativity and problem-solving skills are when starting new businesses. This approach encourages entrepreneurs to start with the resources and capabilities that are available to them and to be creative in finding new opportunities and solutions to problems. For instance, Sara Blakely used her creativity to develop Spanx, a new category of shapewear that addressed a common issue for women and grew into a multi-billion dollar business.

In addition to these theoretical frameworks, there are many real-world examples of how innovation and creativity help entrepreneurs. For example, Steve Jobs's iPod and iPhone changed the music and phone industries by combining technology and design in new and interesting ways. Entrepreneurs like Elon Musk and Jeff Bezos have also used their creativity to start new businesses and opportunities, like space travel and online shopping.

Innovation and creativity are important parts of entrepreneurship. They help entrepreneurs find and take advantage of new opportunities, make customers happy, and grow the economy. Entrepreneurs-to-be can get the skills and mindset they need to succeed in the competitive and ever-changing world of entrepreneurship by understanding the theories and real-world examples of the role of innovation and creativity in entrepreneurship.

Different approaches to entrepreneurship

Over the years, both academics and business people have come up with different ways to approach entrepreneurship. Each approach looks at entrepreneurship from a different angle and focuses on a different part of the process.

> The opportunity-based approach,

which suggests that entrepreneurs identify and pursue opportunities in the market (Shane & Venkataraman, 2000). This approach emphasises the importance of identifying gaps in the market and developing innovative products or services to address those gaps. For example, the founders of Airbnb identified a gap in the market for affordable and convenient accommodations for travellers and developed a platform that connects travellers with hosts who rent out their homes or apartments.

> The resource-based approach,

which suggests that entrepreneurs leverage their resources and capabilities to create value (Barney, 1991). This approach emphasises the importance of identifying and developing resources that can provide a sustainable competitive advantage. For example, the founders of Facebook leveraged their programming skills and social networks to create a platform that connects people around the world and has become one of the most valuable companies in the world.

> The social entrepreneurship approach,

which suggests that entrepreneurs create ventures that address social and environmental issues (Dees, 1998). This approach emphasises the importance of creating social value alongside economic value. For example, Warby Parker is a social enterprise that offers affordable eyeglasses to customers and donates a pair of glasses to someone in need for every pair sold.

> The effective approach,

which suggests that entrepreneurs start with the resources and capabilities they have and experiment with different opportunities (Sarasvathy, 2001). This approach emphasises the importance of creativity, flexibility, and adaptability in entrepreneurship. For example, the founders of Twitter initially developed their platform as a way for individuals to stay in touch with their friends and family but later discovered its potential as a platform for news and information sharing.

These different ways of looking at entrepreneurship give different views on how it works and show different things that make it successful. Entrepreneurs can reach their goals if they understand these different approaches and use them in their businesses.

iii. Identifying and Evaluating Opportunities

Entrepreneurship is all about finding and taking advantage of new or existing markets, technologies, or needs that can be met with new products, services, or solutions. One of the most important parts of entrepreneurship is finding and evaluating opportunities. This section talks about how to find and evaluate opportunities, including the tools, techniques, and frameworks that can be used to figure out whether or not an opportunity will work.

The SWOT analysis is an important tool for finding opportunities. It involves looking at the strengths, weaknesses, opportunities, and threats of a possible business or idea (Humphrey & Memili, 2019). This analysis can help entrepreneurs identify potential challenges and opportunities, and develop strategies to address them. For example, a coffee shop owner may use a SWOT analysis to identify opportunities to expand their menu or open a new location, while also assessing potential challenges such as competition from other coffee shops.

The business model canvas is another important tool for evaluating opportunities. It gives a visual framework for finding key parts of a business model, such as customer segments, value propositions, revenue streams, and cost structures (Osterwalder & Pigneur, 2010). This tool can help business owners figure out which business models are likely to work and which ones have the most potential. It can also help them improve their strategies. For example, a startup that is making a mobile app could use the business model canvas to find possible ways to make money and the costs of making and promoting the app.

Real-world examples of successful entrepreneurship also demonstrate the importance of identifying and evaluating opportunities. For example, the founders of Instagram identified an opportunity to create a social media platform that focused on visual content and capitalised on the growing popularity of smartphones (Gross, 2016). This opportunity ultimately led to the acquisition of Instagram by Facebook for $1 billion. Similarly, the founders of Peloton identified an opportunity to create a new category of exercise equipment and classes that could be accessed from home, rather than at a gym (Shead, 2019). This opportunity has led to the growth of a multi-billion dollar fitness company.

Finding and judging opportunities is a key part of being an entrepreneur. This requires a mix of creativity, knowledge of the market, and analytical skills. By using tools such as the SWOT analysis and business model canvas, and by studying real-world examples of successful entrepreneurship, aspiring entrepreneurs can develop the skills and mindset necessary to identify and capitalise on new opportunities in a rapidly changing business landscape.

How to identify opportunities

Identifying opportunities is a critical step in entrepreneurship, as it allows entrepreneurs to create new products, services, and businesses that meet unmet needs and solve problems. Even though there is no one way to find opportunities, there are a number of strategies and tools that can be used to improve the chances of success.

Aaker, Kumar, and Day (2017) say that one way to find opportunities is to do market research, which involves collecting and analysing data about customer needs, preferences, and behaviours. Market research can help business owners find gaps in the market and come up with products or services to fill them. For example, Fitbit, a company that makes wearable fitness trackers, saw that people wanted more personalised health and fitness data and made a product to meet that need.

Shane (2003) says that another way to find opportunities is to watch how the market and society change. Entrepreneurs can use trends to identify potential areas of growth and innovation. For example, the growth of e-commerce and online shopping has led to the emergence of many new businesses and services, such as meal delivery services and online fashion retailers.

Baker and Nelson (2005) say that entrepreneurs can also find opportunities by drawing on their own experiences and knowledge. Entrepreneurs with experience in a certain industry or field may be able to see unmet needs and opportunities that others have missed. For example, the founder of Patagonia, Yvon Chouinard, was a passionate rock climber and identified a need for high-quality, durable outdoor gear that was not being met by existing companies.

Lastly, Stevenson and Jarillo (1990) say that entrepreneurs can find opportunities by working with other people and sharing ideas. Collaboration can help people come up with new ideas and gain access to new resources and networks. For example, Larry Page and Sergey Brin, the founders of Google, met while they were both getting their master's degrees in computer science. They worked together to create a new search engine that became one of the most valuable companies in the world.

In conclusion, finding opportunities is an important part of being an entrepreneur. It requires creativity, knowledge of the market, and the ability to think strategically. Entrepreneurs can improve their chances of finding and taking advantage of new opportunities by doing things like market research, trend analysis, drawing on their own experiences and knowledge, and working with others.

Market research and analysis

Market research is a critical component of identifying and evaluating opportunities in entrepreneurship. It involves gathering and analysing data about customer needs, preferences, and behaviours to understand the market and identify potential gaps or opportunities (Aaker, Kumar, & Day, 2017). This section explores the process of conducting market research and analysis, including the tools and techniques that can be used to gather and analyse data.

➢ Surveys

One common tool for gathering market data is surveys, which involve asking customers about their needs, preferences, and behaviours (Aaker, Kumar, & Day, 2017). Surveys can be conducted online, through email or social media, or in person. For example, a startup developing a new meal kit delivery service may conduct a survey to understand customers' dietary preferences and meal habits.

➢ Focus Groups

Another tool for gathering market data is focus groups, which involve bringing together a small group of customers to discuss their experiences, preferences, and opinions (Krueger & Casey, 2015). Focus groups can provide in-depth insights into customer needs and preferences, and can help entrepreneurs develop products or services that meet those needs. For example, a startup developing a new clothing line may conduct focus groups to understand customers' style preferences and clothing buying habits.

➢ Data Analysis

Data analysis is also a critical component of market research, as it involves making sense of the data that has been collected and identifying patterns and trends (Aaker, Kumar, & Day, 2017). Data analysis can be done with a number of tools and methods, such as statistical analysis, data visualisation, and predictive modelling. For example, a startup that is making a new mobile app might use predictive modelling to predict how many people will use the app and how often they will use it based on data from the past.

Real-world examples of successful entrepreneurship demonstrate the importance of market research and analysis. For example, Netflix, a company that started as a DVD-by-mail rental service, conducted extensive market research to understand customer preferences and behaviours around video streaming (Sweney, 2014). This research led to the development of a streaming platform that revolutionised the entertainment industry. Similarly, the founders of Dollar Shave Club conducted market research to understand the frustrations customers had with traditional razor buying and developed a subscription-based service that provided affordable, convenient razors delivered directly to customers' doors (Kaplan, 2012).

Market research and analysis is an important part of being an entrepreneur. It requires creativity, analytical skills, and knowledge of the market. Using tools like surveys, focus groups, and techniques for analysing data, entrepreneurs can collect and analyse data to learn about the market and find opportunities for growth and innovation.

Assessing the feasibility of business ideas

Assessing the viability and potential of a business idea is an important part of being an entrepreneur. This is done before time and money are put into developing the idea further. This section talks about how to figure out if a business idea is possible, including the tools, techniques, and frameworks that can be used to look at different parts of the idea.

The lean startup methodology is one way to figure out if a business idea will work. It involves making a minimum viable product (MVP) to test the market and get feedback from customers (Ries, 2011). The lean startup methodology can help entrepreneurs identify potential challenges and opportunities, and develop strategies to address them. For example, Dropbox, a cloud storage company, used the lean startup methodology to develop a minimum viable product and gather feedback from early adopters before scaling their product and business model (Albarran, 2019).

The business model canvas is another way to figure out if a business idea is possible. It gives you a visual way to figure out what the most important parts of a business model are, such as customer segments, value propositions, revenue streams, and cost structures

(Osterwalder & Pigneur, 2010). The business model canvas can help entrepreneurs figure out which business models are likely to work and which ones have the most potential. It can also help them improve their strategies. For example, Airbnb, a company that allows people to rent out their homes or apartments to travellers, used the business model canvas to identify potential revenue streams and costs associated with developing and marketing their platform (Albarran, 2019).

Data analysis is also a key part of figuring out if a business idea is likely to work (Aaker, Kumar, and Day, 2017). This is because it involves making sense of the data that has been collected and finding patterns and trends. Data analysis can be done with a number of tools and methods, such as statistical analysis, data visualisation, and predictive modelling. For example, a startup making a new e-commerce platform might use predictive modelling to predict how many users will use it and how often they will use it based on data from the past.

Real-world examples of successful entrepreneurship show how important it is to figure out if a business idea is possible. For example, Tesla, a company that makes electric cars and clean energy solutions, did a lot of market research and analysis to see if its business idea would work before putting money into production and development (Goodall, 2016). In a similar way, Warby Parker, an online eyewear store, used the lean startup method to create a minimum viable product and get feedback from early adopters before expanding their product line and business model (Albarran, 2019). Also the ride-sharing company Uber used the lean startup methodology to test its minimum viable product and gather feedback from early adopters before scaling its business model (Albarran, 2019). Similarly, the meal delivery service Blue Apron used data analysis to evaluate the feasibility of its business idea and make informed decisions about its growth and development (Kumar, 2017).

Assessing how likely it is that a business idea will work is an important part of being an entrepreneur. This requires a mix of creativity, analytical skills, and market knowledge. By using tools such as the lean startup methodology, business model canvas, and data analysis techniques, entrepreneurs can evaluate the viability and potential of different business ideas and develop strategies to address challenges and opportunities.

iv. Business Planning and Strategy

Business planning and strategy is a critical aspect of entrepreneurship, as it involves developing a plan to achieve specific goals and objectives, and identifying the resources and actions necessary to implement that plan. This section explores the process of business planning and strategy in entrepreneurship, including the tools, frameworks, and techniques that can be used to develop and implement a successful business plan.

The SWOT analysis is a tool for making a business plan. It involves looking at a business idea or venture's strengths, weaknesses, opportunities, and threats (Hill & Westbrook, 1997). The SWOT analysis can help entrepreneurs identify key challenges and opportunities, and develop strategies to address them. For example, a startup developing a new fitness app may use a SWOT analysis to identify potential competitors and develop a strategy to differentiate their product.

The business model canvas is another tool for making a business plan. It gives you a visual way to figure out the most important parts of a business model, such as customer segments, value propositions, revenue streams, and cost structures (Osterwalder & Pigneur, 2010). The business model canvas can help entrepreneurs figure out which business models are likely to work and which ones have the most potential. It can also help them improve their strategies. For example, a startup building a new e-commerce platform could use the business model canvas to figure out how they might make money and how much it will cost to build and market their platform.

Strategy development is also an important part of business planning because it involves figuring out what needs to be done to reach specific goals and objectives and putting them in order of importance (Porter, 1996). There are various frameworks and tools that can be used for strategy development, including the Porter's Five Forces model, which provides a framework for analysing the competitive forces within an industry (Porter, 2008). For example, a startup developing a new software product may use Porter's Five Forces model to analyse the competitive landscape and develop a strategy to differentiate their product and gain market share.

Real-world examples of successful entrepreneurship demonstrate the importance of business planning and strategy. For example, Amazon, a company that started as an online bookseller, developed a business plan that focused on expanding its product offerings and using technology to improve the customer experience (Kim & Mauborgne, 2004). Similarly, Starbucks, a coffee company, developed a strategy that focused on creating a unique customer experience and expanding its product offerings to include food and merchandise (Hill & Jones, 2012).

Business planning and strategy is a critical aspect of entrepreneurship that requires a combination of creativity, analytical skills, and market knowledge. By using tools such as SWOT analysis, the business model canvas, and strategy development frameworks, entrepreneurs can develop and implement successful business plans that help them achieve their goals and objectives.

Developing a business plan

Creating a business plan is a key step in starting a business, as it lays out a plan for how the business will grow and develop. A business plan usually has more than one stage, and each stage has its own goals and content requirements.

Stage 1: Executive Summary

The first stage of a business plan is the executive summary, which is a brief overview of the entire plan. In the executive summary, the business, the target market, the value proposition, and the financial projections should all be briefly explained. (Pinson & Jinnett, 2019) The goal of the executive summary is to give a quick overview of the business that will catch the attention of potential investors and other interested parties.

Stage 2: Company Description

The company description is the second part of a business plan. It gives a detailed overview of the business, including its history, mission, and long-term goals. (Pinson & Jinnett, 2019) The company description should also include information about the company's management team, its legal structure, and any intellectual property or proprietary technology.

Stage 3: Market Analysis

The third stage of a business plan is the market analysis, which involves researching and analysing the target market and the competition. The market analysis should include information on the size and growth potential of the market, the demographics and psychographics of the target customers, and the strengths and weaknesses of the competition. The goal of the market analysis is to find opportunities and threats in the market and come up with a plan to take advantage of those opportunities (Pinson & Jinnett, 2019).

Stage 4: Products and Services

The fourth stage of a business plan is the products and services section, which describes the products or services that the business will offer. This section should include detailed descriptions of the features and benefits of the products or services, as well as any intellectual property or proprietary technology that the business may use. The objective of the products and services section is to demonstrate the value proposition of the business to potential customers (Pinson & Jinnett, 2019).

Stage 5: Marketing and Sales Strategy

The fifth stage of a business plan is the marketing and sales strategy section, which outlines how the business will promote and sell its products or services. This section should include information on the target market, the marketing channels that will be used to reach that market, and the sales strategy that will be used to close deals. In the marketing and sales strategy section, the goal is to show that the business can bring in money and make money (Pinson & Jinnett, 2019).

Stage 6: Financial Projections

The last part of a business plan is the section on financial projections. This section gives detailed information about how the business will do financially. This section should include information about income, expenses, cash flow, profitability, and any assumptions or risks that go along with the financial projections. The goal of the financial projections section is to show that the business is financially viable and to give investors and other interested parties a clear picture of the possible return on investment (Pinson & Jinnett, 2019).

Creating a complete business plan is an important part of being an entrepreneur. This requires a mix of creativity, analytical skills, and knowledge of the market. Entrepreneurs can make and use successful business plans that help them reach their goals and objectives by following the steps outlined above and putting the right information in each section. Tesla and Netflix are two real-world examples of how good business planning and strategy can lead to growth and success.

Setting goals and objectives

Setting goals and objectives is an important part of starting a business because it gives a clear picture of where the business is going and how it will grow. This section explores the importance of setting goals and objectives in entrepreneurship, and the tools and techniques that can be used to set and achieve these goals.

The first step in making goals and objectives for a business is to figure out what its mission and vision are. The mission statement says what the business is for, and the vision statement says what the business should be like in the future (Peng & Dess, 2010). By setting up a clear mission and vision, business owners can set goals and objectives that fit with the business's overall strategy.

Once the mission and vision are clear, entrepreneurs can set goals and objectives that are specific, measurable, achievable, relevant, and time-bound (SMART) (Locke & Latham, 2002). SMART goals and objectives provide a clear and specific framework for achieving success, and can be used to measure progress and make adjustments as necessary.

SMART goals are goals that are clear, measurable, attainable, relevant, and have a time limit. Each element of the SMART acronym has a distinct purpose:

- ➤ Specific: Goals should be specific, clearly defining what is to be achieved and why. Specific goals should be tailored to the mission and vision of the business and should be understood by everyone involved in achieving them.
- ➤ Measurable: Goals should be measurable, allowing for the tracking of progress and evaluation of success. Measurable goals help to ensure that progress is being made towards achieving the desired outcome.
- ➤ Achievable: Goals should be attainable, realistic, and within the business's range of possibilities. Achievable goals are challenging but not impossible, and motivate entrepreneurs to work towards their goals.
- ➤ Relevant: Goals should be relevant, in line with the business's mission and vision, and based on what stakeholders need. Relevant goals should be seen as important to the success of the business.
- ➤ Time-bound: Goals should be time-bound, with a clear timeline for completion. Time-bound goals help to create a

sense of urgency and encourage entrepreneurs to stay focused and on track.

Real-world examples of successful entrepreneurship demonstrate the importance of setting goals and objectives. For example, Google, a company that provides search engine and online advertising services, has a mission to organise the world's information and make it universally accessible and useful (Google, 2022). To achieve this mission, Google has set specific goals and objectives, such as improving search algorithms and developing new products and services, that align with the overall mission and vision of the business.

Another example is Patagonia, a company that designs and sells outdoor apparel and gear, which has a mission to build the best product, cause no unnecessary harm, and use business to inspire and implement solutions to the environmental crisis (Patagonia, 2022). To achieve this mission, Patagonia has set specific goals and objectives, such as reducing its environmental impact and supporting environmental activism, that align with the overall mission and vision of the business.

Setting goals and objectives is an important part of being an entrepreneur and can help business owners reach their vision and mission for the business. By using tools like SMART goals and objectives, business owners can set clear, measurable goals that fit with the business's overall plan. Google and Patagonia are real-world examples of how setting goals and objectives can help a business grow and be successful.

Crafting a business strategy

Crafting a business strategy is a crucial step in entrepreneurship, as it sets the direction and provides a roadmap for the development and growth of a business. This section explores the importance of crafting a business strategy in entrepreneurship and the tools and techniques that can be used to develop an effective strategy.

A business strategy outlines how a company plans to achieve its goals and objectives. It involves identifying the company's strengths and weaknesses, evaluating the market and industry, and developing a plan to achieve a competitive advantage (Porter, 1985). Crafting a business strategy requires careful analysis and planning to ensure that the strategy is viable and achievable.

Entrepreneurs can use different strategies to gain an edge over their competitors, such as:

> Cost Leadership Strategy:

A cost leadership strategy is to make and sell products or services at a lower price than competitors while keeping the same level of quality. Businesses that compete in price-sensitive markets frequently employ this strategy (Porter, 1985).

> Differentiation Strategy:

A differentiation strategy means making products or services that are different from those of competitors and that people want. Businesses that compete in markets with fierce competition and clients who place a high value on quality, features, or services frequently employ this strategy (Porter, 1985).

> Focus Strategy:

Focusing on a certain part of the market and making products or services fit the needs and preferences of that part is what a focus strategy is. Businesses that cater to specialised or distinctive customer needs that are unmet by larger companies frequently employ this tactic (Porter, 1985).

> Best-Cost Provider Strategy:

A best-cost provider strategy is to offer products or services that are both cheaper than those of competitors and of higher quality. This strategy is often used by businesses that target customers that are value-conscious and seek high-quality products or services at an affordable price (Kozlenkova et al., 2014).

> Focus Differentiation Strategy:

Focusing on a specific part of the market and making products or services fit the needs and preferences of that part is a focus differentiation strategy. This is a common strategy for small businesses that meet specific or unique customer needs that larger companies don't meet. (Porter, 1985).

> Blue Ocean Strategy:

A blue ocean strategy involves creating a new market space where competition is irrelevant, and demand is created by offering a unique product or service that does not currently exist in the market. This strategy is often used by businesses that seek to disrupt an existing market or create a new one altogether (Kim & Mauborgne, 2005).

> Growth Strategy:

As part of a growth strategy, a business may increase sales, move into new markets or product lines, or buy other businesses. Businesses that want to grow their market share and make more money often use this method (Ansoff, 1957).

> Diversification Strategy:

A strategy for diversification is to grow the business into new markets or product lines that have nothing to do with the current business. Businesses that want to reduce risk and make more money often use this method (Ansoff, 1957).

> Mergers and Acquisitions Strategy:

A mergers and acquisitions strategy involves buying or merging with another business to increase market share, reduce competition, or get access to new markets or technologies. This is a strategy that businesses often use when they want to grow quickly (Gaughan, 2010).

> Innovation Strategy:

A strategy for innovation is to come up with new products or services, technologies, or business models that give customers something they can't get anywhere else. Businesses that want to stay ahead of the competition and open up new markets frequently employ this strategy (Christensen, 1997).

Entrepreneurs can use a variety of tools and methods, such as SWOT analysis, PESTEL analysis, and Porter's Five Forces analysis (Johnson et al., 2008), to come up with a business strategy. These tools can help entrepreneurs identify the strengths, weaknesses, opportunities, and threats of their business, as well as the external factors that may impact the success of the business.

Real-world examples of successful entrepreneurship demonstrate the importance of crafting a business strategy. For example, Nike, a company that designs and sells athletic footwear and apparel, has a business strategy that focuses on innovation, sustainability, and customer experience (Nike, 2022). To achieve this strategy, Nike has developed new products and technologies, implemented sustainable practices throughout its supply chain, and focused on providing exceptional customer service and experiences.

Another example is Starbucks, a company that sells coffee and related products, which has a business strategy that focuses on differentiation and creating a unique customer experience (Starbucks, 2022). To achieve this strategy, Starbucks has developed high-quality products, a unique store atmosphere, and a customer loyalty program.

Creating a business strategy is an important part of being an entrepreneur because it can help them reach their goals. By using tools such as SWOT analysis, PESTEL analysis, and Porter's Five

Forces analysis, entrepreneurs can develop a strategy that is viable and achievable, and that aligns with the overall mission and vision of the business. Different strategies, such as cost leadership, differentiation, focus, best-cost provider, and blue ocean, may be implemented to achieve a competitive advantage. Real-world examples such as Nike and Starbucks demonstrate the effectiveness of these strategies in achieving success in highly competitive industries.

v. Financing Your Venture

Financing your business is an important part of being an entrepreneur because it means getting the money you need to start and grow your business. Entrepreneurs have many ways to get money, such as using their own money, crowdsourcing, angel investing, venture capital, and getting loans from banks or other financial institutions. Each choice has its own pros and cons, so it's important to think carefully about your business's needs and goals before making a decision.

In this section, we'll talk about the different ways entrepreneurs can get money, as well as their pros and cons. We will also show you how to make a good financial plan, including making financial projections, making a budget, and managing cash flow. We will also talk about how to get ready for meetings with potential investors, such as how to make a convincing pitch and explain your business idea in a clear and concise way.

Understanding financing options

Entrepreneurs need to know about the different ways they can get the money they need to start and grow their businesses. (Berger & Udell, 2006) says that there are two main types of financing: debt financing and equity financing.

Borrowing money from a lender and paying it back with interest over a certain amount of time is called debt financing. Debt financing is a common way for small businesses to pay for their operations, buy inventory, or buy equipment or machinery. Traditional bank loans, lines of credit, and credit cards are all ways to pay off debt.

Equity financing, on the other hand, is when you sell a piece of your business in exchange for money. Businesses that are brand-new or experiencing rapid growth and require a lot of capital typically use equity financing. Angel investors, venture capitalists, and crowdfunding are all types of equity financing (Hornuf & Schwienbacher, 2018).

Both debt financing and equity financing have their own pros and cons, and business owners need to carefully weigh their options before choosing the best one for their business.

Debt financing provides entrepreneurs with access to funds that they can use to run their business, without having to give up ownership or control of the company. However, debt financing comes with the risk of defaulting on the loan, which can lead to high interest rates, fees, and damage to the entrepreneur's credit score.

On the other hand, equity financing gives business owners access to large amounts of money that can be used to grow the business. In addition, equity financing can bring in experienced investors who can help with mentorship, advice, and connections to other professionals in the same field. However, equity financing also means giving up a portion of ownership and control of the business, and investors may have different goals or priorities for the company than the entrepreneur.

In the end, entrepreneurs need to know about the different financing options they have in order to make smart decisions about how to fund their business. Entrepreneurs should consider their business needs, goals, and priorities, and seek professional advice when necessary to determine the most appropriate financing option for their specific situation (U.S. Small Business Administration, 2022).

Raising capital

Many entrepreneurs have a hard time getting enough money to start their businesses, but there are several ways they can do it. Here are some of the most common methods:

> ➤ Bootstrapping:

One of the most straightforward methods of raising capital is to use personal savings or resources to finance the business. This method is known as bootstrapping, and it allows entrepreneurs to maintain control and ownership of their companies. However, it may not provide enough capital for significant growth. One successful example of bootstrapping is Mailchimp, a marketing automation platform that was self-funded for over a decade before raising its first round of venture capital (Rao, 2020).

> ➤ Debt Financing:

Borrowing money from lenders or investors and paying back the loans with interest over time is a form of debt financing. This method is beneficial for businesses that need capital for short-term expenses or have a steady cash flow. A successful example of debt financing is Ben & Jerry's, which started as a small ice cream shop and later secured a loan to expand its operations. Unilever later purchased the business for $326 million after it eventually went public (Mackey, 2020).

> Equity Financing:

Equity financing is when a company sells a piece of itself to investors in exchange for money. This method provides significant capital for growth, but requires giving up ownership and control of the business to the investors. One successful example of equity financing is Airbnb, which raised $7.2 million in seed funding from several investors, including Sequoia Capital and Greylock Partners, before becoming a global hospitality giant valued at over $100 billion (Chen, 2020).

> Crowdfunding:

Crowdfunding is a relatively new method of raising capital, where entrepreneurs can solicit funding from a large number of individuals through online platforms. One successful example of crowdfunding is Oculus VR, a virtual reality company that raised $2.4 million on Kickstarter in 2012 before being acquired by Facebook for $2 billion in 2014 (Geron, 2014).

Entrepreneurs have several options for raising capital, each with its own advantages and disadvantages. It is important for entrepreneurs to carefully consider their options and develop a comprehensive financing plan that aligns with their business goals and objectives.

Managing finances

Once a business has gotten the money it needs, it needs to manage its money well to be successful in the long run. This involves creating a budget, tracking expenses and revenue, and making strategic financial decisions.

Creating a budget that shows how much it costs to run the business is an important part of managing money. This includes expenses such as rent, salaries, utilities, and equipment. A budget can help entrepreneurs stay on track with their spending and identify areas where they can cut costs or reallocate resources (Adidam et al., 2006).

Another important aspect of managing finances is tracking expenses and revenue. This involves keeping accurate records of all financial transactions and regularly reviewing financial statements to ensure the business is operating within its budget and generating enough revenue to cover expenses. One useful tool for tracking finances is accounting software, such as QuickBooks or Xero (Stewart & Zhao, 2000).

Making strategic financial decisions is also crucial for the long-term success of a business. This may involve decisions about investing in new equipment or technology, expanding into new markets, or hiring additional staff. Entrepreneurs should carefully evaluate the potential costs and benefits of these decisions before making any major financial commitments (Bhide, 1994).

Here are some best practices for managing finances:

➢ Create a realistic budget:

A budget is a crucial tool for managing finances. Entrepreneurs should create a realistic budget that accurately reflects the costs of running the business, including expenses such as rent, salaries, utilities, and equipment. It's important to regularly review the budget and adjust it as needed to ensure the business is operating within its means (Adidam et al., 2006).

➢ Keep accurate financial records:

It's important to keep accurate records of all financial transactions, including receipts, invoices, and bank statements. This will help entrepreneurs track expenses and revenue, and identify areas where they can cut costs or reallocate resources. Accounting software, such as QuickBooks or Xero, can be a useful tool for tracking finances (Stewart & Zhao, 2000).

➤ Make strategic financial decisions:
Entrepreneurs should think carefully about the costs and benefits of any big financial decisions, like buying new equipment or technology, expanding into new markets, or hiring more people. Entrepreneurs can make sure their businesses are set up for long-term growth by making smart financial decisions (Bhide, 1994).

Failure to effectively manage finances can have serious consequences for a business, including:

➤ Cash flow problems: Poor financial management can lead to cash flow problems, which can make it difficult to pay bills and meet financial obligations.
➤ Opportunities lost: If a business doesn't plan its finances well, it might miss out on chances to invest in new projects, grow into new markets, or hire more people.
➤ Legal problems: If you don't manage your money well, you could end up with tax problems or a fight with a creditor.

Effective financial management is critical for the success of a business. By creating a realistic budget, keeping accurate financial records, and making strategic financial decisions, entrepreneurs can ensure their businesses are financially healthy and positioned for long-term growth.

vi. Building a Strong Team

Building a strong team is essential for the success of any business. Entrepreneurs need to identify and recruit the right people to help them achieve their goals. This involves creating job descriptions, developing a hiring process, and providing ongoing training and support to team members.

One of the key components of building a strong team is creating job descriptions that clearly define the roles and responsibilities of each team member. This helps ensure that everyone understands their role and can work together effectively to achieve the business's goals.

Building a strong team also means coming up with a way to hire people who are the best at what they do. Barrick, Mount, and Li (2013) say that this can be done by posting job openings on job boards, making connections with people in the industry, and giving candidates thorough interviews to figure out if they have the right skills and fit with the company's culture.

It's also important to give team members ongoing training and support if you want to build a strong team. This can help team members develop new skills and stay up-to-date with the latest industry trends, as well as improve their performance and job satisfaction (Tims, Bakker, & Derks, 2013).

Real-world examples of successful businesses that have built strong teams include Apple, Google, and Amazon. (Morgeson & Campion, 2003) These companies have been able to hire and keep top talent because they offer competitive salaries and benefits, create a good work environment, and offer ongoing training and development opportunities.

Building a strong team is critical for the success of any business. By creating job descriptions, developing a hiring process, and providing ongoing training and support to team members, entrepreneurs can ensure they have the right people in place to help them achieve their goals.

Hiring the right people

Hiring the right people is essential for the success of any business. Entrepreneurs need to identify and recruit individuals who have the necessary skills, experience, and values to help them achieve their goals.

One of the first steps in hiring the right people is creating job descriptions that accurately reflect the skills and qualifications required for each role. This can help get the right people to apply and make sure they know what the job entails and what is expected of them (Barrick, Mount, & Li, 2013).

During the hiring process, candidates should also be carefully judged on their skills and how well they fit in with the company's culture. This may involve conducting interviews, reviewing resumes and cover letters, and checking references. It's important to take the time to carefully evaluate each candidate to ensure that they have the skills and experience needed to succeed in the role (Maurer, 2016).

Another important aspect of hiring the right people is considering diversity and inclusion. By actively seeking out candidates from diverse backgrounds and creating an inclusive hiring process, entrepreneurs can build a more effective and innovative team (Pitts, Hicklin, & Hawes, 2018).

Last but not least, it's important for the success of the business and the success of the new hires to give them ongoing training and support. This can help them develop new skills and integrate into the company culture, as well as improve their job satisfaction and performance (Tims, Bakker, & Derks, 2013).

Effective hiring practices have been shown to be a key driver of business success. For example, a study by McKinsey & Company found that companies with more diverse workforces are more likely to outperform their less diverse peers (Hunt, Layton, & Prince, 2015).

Hiring the right people is essential for the success of any business. By creating accurate job descriptions, conducting thorough assessments, considering diversity and inclusion, and providing ongoing training and support, entrepreneurs can build a strong and effective team.

Motivating and managing employees

Motivating and managing employees is critical for the success of any business. Entrepreneurs need to create a work environment that fosters employee engagement, productivity, and satisfaction. This involves setting clear expectations, providing regular feedback, and recognising employees for their contributions.

One of the key components of motivating and managing employees is setting clear expectations. Employees need to understand what is expected of them in terms of their roles and responsibilities, as well as the goals and objectives of the business. This can help them stay focused and aligned with the overall mission of the company (Locke & Latham, 2013).

Providing regular feedback is also essential for motivating and managing employees. This can help employees understand how they are performing and identify areas for improvement. Feedback should be specific, timely, and constructive, and should focus on both strengths and areas for improvement (Kluger & DeNisi, 1996).

Recognising employees for their contributions is another important aspect of motivating and managing employees. This can help increase employee engagement and job satisfaction, as well as promote a positive work culture. Recognition can come in many forms, including bonuses, promotions, and public praise (Gallup, 2017).

Management and motivation of employees that work well have been linked to higher levels of productivity, job satisfaction, and profits. For example, a study by Gallup found that companies with engaged employees have higher earnings per share than their less engaged peers (Gallup, 2017).

Best practices employee motivation:

> Set clear goals and expectations for employees (Locke & Latham, 2013).
> Provide regular feedback and coaching to employees (Kluger & DeNisi, 1996).
> Recognise and reward employees for their contributions (Gallup, 2017).
> Foster a positive work culture that promotes teamwork and collaboration (Gittell, Seidner, & Wimbush, 2010).
> Provide opportunities for professional growth and development (Weiner, 2013).
> (Luthans & Yousef, 2007) Make sure that employees have the tools and help they need to do their jobs well.
> Promote work-life balance and well-being (Rashid, Sambasivan, & Johari, 2013).
> Encourage open communication and transparency (Edmondson, 2012).
> Lead by example and set a positive tone at the top (Goleman, Boyatzis, & McKee, 2013).

➤ Vroom and Jago (2007) say that you should always look at how your employee motivation strategies are working and make changes based on feedback and results.

(Gallup, 2017; Gittell et al., 2010; Luthans & Youssef, 2007) have found that these best practises are linked to more motivated, engaged, and happy employees, as well as better business results.

Motivating and managing employees is essential for the success of any business. By setting clear expectations, providing regular feedback, and recognising employees for their contributions, entrepreneurs can build a motivated and engaged team that is aligned with the overall mission of the company.

Building a positive company culture

For a business to be successful and last, it needs to have a good company culture. A good company culture helps to find and keep good employees, boosts morale, and creates a sense of community and teamwork within the company. In this section, we'll look at some ways to build a good company culture and the benefits of doing so, based on research in this area.

A strong set of values that guide the mission and operations of the company is one of the most important parts of a good company culture. Research has shown that companies with a clear and well-defined set of values tend to have more engaged and committed employees (Denison, 1990). Companies can foster a strong set of values by involving employees in the development of the company's mission statement and core values and ensuring that these values are reflected in all aspects of the organisation's operations.

Another important element of a positive company culture is effective communication. Regular and transparent communication helps to build trust and foster a sense of community within the organisation. Leaders can encourage effective communication by establishing regular channels for feedback, implementing an open-door policy, and regularly communicating company updates and news to all employees (Berson et al., 2019).

Recognition and rewards are also important for building a positive company culture. Employees who feel valued and appreciated are more likely to be engaged and motivated. Companies can recognise and reward employees through regular performance evaluations, employee of the month awards, and other incentives. In addition, fostering a culture of celebration and recognition of accomplishments can help to build a sense of pride and community within the organisation (Kim & Organ, 2018).

Finally, creating a positive work environment is crucial for building a positive company culture. This includes providing employees with the necessary resources and tools to do their job effectively, as well as creating a welcoming and inclusive workplace that respects and values diversity. Companies can create a positive work environment by implementing flexible work arrangements, offering opportunities for career development and training, and promoting work-life balance (Garca-Sánchez et al., 2019).

For a business to be successful and last, it needs to have a good company culture. Some ways to build a good company culture are to create a strong set of values, communicate well, give recognition and rewards, and make the workplace a good place to be. By fostering a positive company culture, businesses can attract and retain employees, boost morale, and create a sense of community and collaboration within the organisation.

vii. Marketing and Sales

Marketing and sales are critical components of any successful business. Entrepreneurs need to understand the needs and preferences of their target customers, and create marketing and sales strategies that effectively reach and engage them.

This part will talk about things like researching and analysing the market, branding, advertising, and sales techniques. It will also discuss the importance of creating a strong value proposition, and building long-term relationships with customers.

Kotler and Keller (2016) found that when marketing and sales are done well, customer satisfaction, brand loyalty, and profits go up. For example, a study by Bain & Company found that increasing customer retention rates by just 5% can increase profits by 25% to 95% (Bain & Company, 2019).

In the sections that follow, we'll talk about marketing and sales best practises and strategies, as well as real-world examples of companies that have used these techniques successfully.

Creating a marketing plan

A marketing plan is a roadmap for achieving marketing goals and objectives. It outlines the strategies and tactics that a business will use to reach its target customers and promote its products or services.

The following are the key stages in creating a comprehensive marketing plan:

➤ Conduct market research and analysis:
The first step in making a marketing plan is to do a thorough analysis of the target market, including the needs and wants of customers, the size of the market, and the companies that are already in it. Kotler et al. (2017) say that this information can be found through either primary research (like surveys or focus groups) or secondary research (like industry reports or online databases).

➤ Define target customers and positioning:
After doing a market analysis, the next step is to figure out who your target customers are and how to position your business. This

involves identifying the unique value proposition that the business offers, and how it can differentiate itself from competitors in the eyes of target customers (Kotler et al., 2017).

> Set marketing goals and objectives:

Once the target customers and positioning have been defined, the next step is to set specific marketing goals and objectives. (Kotler et al., 2017) Some of these are building brand awareness, getting leads, and driving sales.

> Develop marketing strategies and tactics:

Based on the marketing goals and objectives, the next step is to come up with marketing strategies and tactics that will help the target customers be reached and engaged. Kotler et al. (2017) say that this can include branding, advertising, public relations, social media, events, and other ways to get the word out.

> Allocate resources and set a budget:

After coming up with marketing strategies and plans, the next step is to decide how to spend money and what resources to use. This means figuring out how many people, what kind of equipment, and how much money will be spent on marketing to make the plan work (Kotler et al., 2017).

➤ Implement the plan and measure results:

The final step in creating a marketing plan is to implement the strategies and tactics, and track and measure the results. This may involve analysing website traffic, social media engagement, sales metrics, or other key performance indicators (Kotler et al., 2017).

Creating a comprehensive marketing plan can help entrepreneurs to effectively reach and engage their target customers, and ultimately drive business growth and profitability.

Understanding target markets

Target markets are specific groups of customers that a business aims to reach and serve with its products or services. To create effective marketing strategies and get customers involved, it's important to find and understand your target markets.

The following are some examples of target markets:

➤ Geographic target markets:

This means customers in a certain city, region, or country. Kotler et al. (2017) say that a local bakery might try to reach customers within a 10-mile radius.

➢ Demographic target markets:

This means customers who fit a certain profile, such as their age, gender, income, or level of education. For example, a luxury fashion brand may target high-income customers aged 25-45 years old (Kotler et al., 2017).

➢ Psychographic target markets:

This refers to customers with specific lifestyle, personality, or value-based characteristics. For example, a health food company may target customers who prioritise healthy living and sustainability (Kotler et al., 2017).

➢ Behavioural target markets:

This means customers who have certain habits or preferences, like buying a lot, being loyal to a certain brand, or shopping based on price. Kotler et al. (2017) say that a grocery store might try to attract customers who often buy organic food.

To create marketing messages and promotional strategies that resonate with customers and get them involved, it's important to know what makes target markets unique and what they like.

Developing a sales strategy

A sales strategy is a plan that shows how a business will find, attract, and keep customers to reach its sales goals. To make a good sales strategy, you need to know your target market, find the best sales channels, and tailor your messages and strategies to the needs and preferences of your customers.

The following are some different types of sales strategies:

➤ Direct sales:

This means selling directly to customers in person, over the phone, or through online sales channels. Direct sales can work well for businesses that sell high-value, complicated products or services that need a consultative sales approach (Ingram, 2022).

➤ Indirect sales:

This involves selling through intermediaries such as distributors, wholesalers, or retailers. Indirect sales can be effective for businesses that want to expand their reach and access new markets, but may have lower profit margins (Ingram, 2022).

➤ Inside sales:

This involves selling remotely, often through phone, email, or video conferencing. Inside sales can be effective for businesses that want to reduce travel costs and reach customers in different geographic locations (Ingram, 2022).

➤ Account-based sales:

This means going after specific high-value customers or accounts and making sure that your sales strategies and messages are tailored to their needs and preferences. (Germann, Ebbes, & Grewal, 2021) Account-based sales can work well for businesses that offer high-value, customised products or services.

➤ Relationship sales:

This involves building long-term relationships with customers through ongoing communication, support, and engagement. Relationship sales can be effective for businesses that want to build customer loyalty and repeat business (Germann, Ebbes, & Grewal, 2021).

Businesses can reach their sales goals and build long-term relationships with customers by making a sales strategy that fits the needs and preferences of their target customers.

viii. Scaling and Growth

Scaling a business means growing its size, income, and reach while keeping its efficiency and profitability. Scaling naturally leads to growth, which usually means entering new markets, making new products or services, and getting more customers. Achieving sustainable growth requires careful planning, strategic decision-making, and effective execution.

The following are some key considerations for scaling and growing a business:

> Setting up a strong base: Before scaling, it's important to make sure the business has a solid base in terms of finances, operations, and organisational structure. This may involve improving processes, investing in technology, or building a strong team.

> Finding growth opportunities: This means doing research and analysis on the market to find new markets, products, or services that could help the business grow. This may involve

expanding geographically, diversifying product lines, or targeting new customer segments.

- ➤ Developing a growth strategy: This involves creating a plan that outlines how the business will achieve its growth goals. The strategy could involve making new partnerships, putting money into marketing and advertising, or opening up more channels of distribution.

- ➤ Using resources well: As a business grows, it is important to use resources well to keep making money and running efficiently. This may involve investing in new technology, hiring additional staff, or outsourcing certain tasks.

- ➤ Measuring and evaluating performance: It's important to do this on a regular basis to make sure the business is meeting its growth goals. This could mean keeping an eye on key performance indicators (KPIs), surveying customers, or looking at financial statements.

Successful examples of businesses that have scaled and grown include companies such as Amazon, Google, and Facebook. These businesses have grown by getting into new markets, making new products and services, and using technology to help them grow.

Managing growth

Managing growth is the process of making sure that a business can keep running and making money even as it grows and scales. This involves developing strategies and processes that can accommodate increased demand, while also maintaining quality, efficiency, and customer satisfaction.

The following are some different types of growth strategies:

- ➤ Organic growth is when a business grows by using its own resources and methods, like making new products or services, entering new markets, or putting more effort into marketing and advertising (Kotler et al., 2017).
- ➤ Strategic partnerships involve forming alliances or partnerships with other businesses to share resources, increase reach, or create new products or services (Mullins & Komisar, 2019).
- ➤ Merger and acquisition (M&A) means buying or merging with other businesses to get access to new markets, customers, or resources (Mullins & Komisar, 2019).

- (Kotler et al., 2017) Franchising is when the business model and brand are licenced to other entrepreneurs who run their own businesses under the brand name.
- Licensing: This involves granting other businesses the right to use the company's intellectual property, such as patents, trademarks, or copyrights, in exchange for royalties or fees (Kotler et al., 2017).

Effective management of growth requires careful planning and execution, as well as the ability to adapt to changing market conditions and customer needs. Businesses that successfully manage growth can achieve sustained profitability and competitive advantage in their industries.

Growth Mismanagement

While growth is typically seen as a positive outcome for businesses, it can also lead to mismanagement if not properly planned and executed. Growth mismanagement can occur in several ways, including:

- Overexpansion: Rapid growth can lead to strained resources, insufficient cash flow, and a lack of focus on core business activities, which can lead to failure (Sahlman, 2012).

- Lack of focus: Businesses that try to do too many things at once can suffer from a lack of focus, resulting in decreased efficiency, quality, and customer satisfaction (McGrath, 2013).

- Ineffective leadership: As a company grows, the leadership team may find it hard to keep the culture and values that led to the company's success, which can lower employee morale and cause more people to leave (Kotter, 2012).

- Poor financial management: As a business grows, it gets harder to handle money well, which can lead to problems with cash flow, debt, and even bankruptcy (Mullins & Komisar, 2019).

To avoid mismanaging growth, businesses need to have a clear plan for growth, use their resources well, and focus on their core business activities. Regular monitoring and evaluation of performance can also help businesses identify and address growth mismanagement issues before they become significant problems.

Expanding your business

Expanding a business is an exciting opportunity, but it also comes with risks and challenges. Businesses need to have a clear plan, use their resources well, and carefully manage growth if they want to grow.

The following are some key steps to consider when expanding your business:

1. Develop a growth strategy. Businesses need to figure out the best ways to grow, like opening new locations, entering new markets, or making new products or services (Kotler et al., 2017).

2. Allocate resources effectively: Expanding a business requires significant resources, including capital, talent, and time. Businesses need to plan and allocate resources effectively to achieve their growth goals (Mullins & Komisar, 2019).

3. Manage risk: There are risks that come with growing a business, such as more competition, changing market conditions, and unexpected costs. (Mullins & Komisar, 2019) To deal with these risks, businesses need to make

backup plans and regularly check on and evaluate their performance.

4. Maintain customer satisfaction: As businesses grow, it can be hard for them to keep the high level of customer satisfaction that got them where they are today. Businesses need to focus on providing quality products and services, as well as developing strong relationships with customers (Kotler et al., 2017).

5. Foster a strong company culture. As businesses grow, it can be hard for them to keep the same culture and values that made them successful in the first place. (Kotter, 2012) says that businesses need to build and support a strong company culture to keep employee morale and productivity high.

Effective expansion requires careful planning and execution, as well as the ability to adapt to changing market conditions and customer needs. Businesses that successfully expand can achieve increased profitability, market share, and competitive advantage in their industries.

Expanding a business can be a challenging process, but it can also lead to increased profits, brand awareness, and customer loyalty. One example of a business that has successfully expanded its operations is Starbucks.

Starbucks started as a single store in Seattle, Washington, in 1971. The company initially focused on selling coffee beans and equipment, but soon expanded into selling brewed coffee, pastries, and other food items. In the 1990s, Starbucks began to expand rapidly, opening new stores across the United States and internationally (Gamble & Thompson, 2020).

To support this growth, Starbucks developed several key strategies, including:

- ➢ Product diversification: Starbucks started selling more than just coffee. It started selling tea, snacks, and other food items in addition to coffee.
- ➢ International expansion: Starbucks went global by entering new markets and adapting its products and marketing to the tastes and preferences of people in those places.
- ➢ Brand management: Starbucks kept a consistent brand image across all of its stores, which made the Starbucks name easy to recognise and trust.
- ➢ Technology adoption: Starbucks used technology to make their business run more smoothly and make the customer experience better. They did this by putting in place mobile

ordering and payment systems and digital rewards programmes (Gamble & Thompson, 2020). Through these strategies, Starbucks has been able to maintain its position as a leading global coffee retailer, with over 31,000 stores in 82 countries (Starbucks Corporation, 2022).

Scaling operations

Scaling operations means increasing the amount of products or services a business can sell while keeping or improving quality and efficiency. To scale operations successfully, businesses need to consider the following factors:

> Streamline processes: As businesses grow, processes can become more complex and time-consuming. Streamlining processes can help increase efficiency and productivity, which is essential for scaling operations (Osterwalder & Pigneur, 2010).

> Automate where possible: Automation can help businesses save time and reduce costs, which is important for scaling operations. Brynjolfsson and McAfee (2014) say that automation can include using software to run operations,

using robots or machines to do tasks, or giving customers ways to help themselves.

➢ Develop a supply chain: A reliable supply chain is essential for scaling operations. Businesses need to identify suppliers, develop relationships with them, and implement processes to manage inventory and delivery (Slack et al., 2017).

➢ Monitor and evaluate performance: Regular monitoring and evaluation of performance is essential for scaling operations. This can involve tracking key performance indicators (KPIs), conducting customer surveys, and analysing financial data to identify areas for improvement (Mullins & Komisar, 2019).

➢ Invest in talent: As businesses scale operations, they will need to hire additional staff to manage increased demand. Investing in talent by hiring skilled and experienced employees and providing ongoing training and development is essential for maintaining quality and efficiency (Kotter, 2012).

Businesses can increase their ability to sell products or services, reach new markets, and have long-term success if they know how to scale their operations well.

ix. Managing Risk and Uncertainty

Entrepreneurship involves inherent risks and uncertainties that can impact a business's success. To effectively manage risk and uncertainty, entrepreneurs need to develop strategies to identify, assess, and mitigate potential threats.

The following are some key steps to consider when managing risk and uncertainty:

> Identify possible risks: Businesses need to look for risks that could affect their operations, such as changes in the economy, changes in the market, and legal problems (Mullins & Komisar, 2019).

> Assess the likelihood and impact of risks. Once potential risks have been found, businesses need to figure out how likely each one is to happen and how bad it will be if it does. Mullins and Komisar (2019) say that this can be done by using tools like risk matrices or scenario analysis to figure out what each risk might mean.

- ➢ Develop contingency plans: Contingency plans are essential for managing risk and uncertainty. Businesses need to develop plans to address potential threats, such as developing a crisis management plan or creating a backup supply chain (Kotler et al., 2017).

- ➢ Monitor and evaluate risks: It's important to keep an eye on risks and evaluate them often in order to deal with risk and uncertainty. (Mullins & Komisar, 2019) This can involve looking at financial data, keeping an eye on customer trends, and doing market research to find possible threats.

- ➢ Change with the times. Being an entrepreneur means dealing with constant change and uncertainty, and businesses need to be able to change with the times. (Osterwalder & Pigneur, 2010) This can mean changing the business model, the marketing strategy, or the product or service being offered.

Effective risk management is essential for the long-term success of a business. By identifying potential risks, assessing their likelihood and impact, developing contingency plans, and adapting to changing circumstances, entrepreneurs can mitigate potential threats and improve their chances of success.

Identifying and managing risks

Entrepreneurship involves inherent risks and uncertainties that can impact a business's success. To effectively manage risk and uncertainty, entrepreneurs need to develop strategies to identify, assess, and mitigate potential threats.

Identifying Risks

The first step in managing risk is to figure out what risks the business might face. This can be done by doing a SWOT analysis (strengths, weaknesses, opportunities, and threats) to find potential risks and opportunities (Kuratko & Hornsby, 2017).

Common types of risks include:

- Market risks: such as changes in consumer behaviour or increased competition
- Operational risks: such as equipment failure or supply chain disruption
- Financial risks: such as changes in interest rates or economic downturns
- Legal and regulatory risks: such as changes in laws or compliance issues

Assessing and Managing Risks

Once possible risks have been found, businesses need to figure out how likely and bad each one is. Mullins and Komisar (2019) say that this can be done by using tools like risk matrices or scenario analysis to figure out what each risk might mean.

After assessing risks, businesses need to develop strategies to manage them. This can include developing contingency plans to address potential threats, such as developing a crisis management plan or creating a backup supply chain (Kotler et al., 2017). It is also important to regularly monitor and evaluate risks to ensure that the business is prepared to adapt to changing circumstances (Mullins & Komisar, 2019).

Consequences of Poor Risk Management

Poor risk management can cost a business a lot of money, hurt its reputation, and get it into trouble with the law, among other things. For example, the global financial crisis of 2008 was caused in large part by the way banks handled risk (Cohen, 2015).

Effective risk management can help businesses to mitigate potential threats and improve their chances of success.

Dealing with uncertainty

Entrepreneurship involves operating in an environment of uncertainty, where businesses may face unexpected challenges and changes in the market or industry. To effectively manage uncertainty, entrepreneurs need to be prepared to adapt and pivot their strategies as needed.

Building Flexibility

One way to manage uncertainty is to build flexibility into the business model. This can involve developing contingency plans and creating a culture of agility and adaptability (Blank & Dorf, 2012).

Entrepreneurs can also use lean startup methods, which focus on quick experiments and feedback from customers to quickly improve products or services (Ries, 2011).

Scenario Planning

Scenario planning is another way for businesses to deal with uncertainty. In this method, businesses come up with a number of possible scenarios and plans for how to handle each one (Schoemaker, 1995).

This can mean thinking about a range of possible outcomes and coming up with plans for each one. Businesses can be better ready to adapt and respond to changes in the market or industry if they plan for different possible outcomes.

Collaboration and Networking

Collaboration and networking can also be valuable strategies for managing uncertainty. By building relationships with other businesses and entrepreneurs, businesses can access new ideas and resources and develop partnerships to help weather uncertain times (Isenberg, 2010).

Consequences of Poor Uncertainty Management

If you don't handle uncertainty well, you might miss opportunities and be unable to adapt to changing situations, which can hurt the success of your business. For example, Kodak didn't adapt well to the change from film to digital photography, which led to a loss of market share and, in the end, bankruptcy (Christensen, 1997).

Effective management of uncertainty can help businesses to identify and capitalise on new opportunities and navigate unexpected challenges.

Preparing for unforeseen circumstances

Even though uncertainty is a part of being an entrepreneur, there are things that entrepreneurs can do to prepare for the unexpected and lessen the effects of problems that come up out of the blue.

Contingency Planning

One key strategy for preparing for unforeseen circumstances is contingency planning. This involves developing backup plans and contingencies for potential risks and challenges that may arise in the business (Snyder & Duarte, 2006).

Identifying possible risks and problems, making plans to deal with those problems, and regularly reviewing and updating those plans to make sure they are still useful are all parts of contingency planning.

Financial Planning

Another important aspect of preparing for unforeseen circumstances is financial planning. This can involve building up reserves or emergency funds to help weather unexpected challenges and changes in the market (Wang, Walker, & Redmond, 2016).

Entrepreneurs can also think about making financial models to help them plan for and prepare for possible financial problems and changes in the market.

Insurance

Insurance is another tool that entrepreneurs can use to prepare for unforeseen circumstances. This can include business interruption insurance, which can provide financial assistance in the event of unexpected disruptions to the business (Levene & Henriques, 2017).

Entrepreneurs should look over their insurance options carefully and think about which policies are best for their business.

Consequences of Poor Preparation

Poor preparation for unforeseen circumstances can leave businesses vulnerable to unexpected challenges and disruptions. This can impact a business's ability to continue operations, as well as its financial stability and overall success.

Effective preparation can help businesses to weather unexpected challenges and continue operations, even in the face of unforeseen circumstances.

x. Entrepreneurship and Society

Entrepreneurship has a big effect on society because it helps the economy grow, creates jobs, and leads to new ideas (Santos & Eisenhardt, 2009). As such, it is important to understand the relationship between entrepreneurship and society.

The Role of Entrepreneurship in Economic Development

Entrepreneurship plays a key role in driving economic growth and development (Audretsch, 2015). This is particularly true for small and medium-sized enterprises (SMEs), which are often seen as the backbone of many economies.

(Stam, 2015) Entrepreneurship can lead to more jobs, more competition, and the growth of new industries and markets. Entrepreneurship can also help encourage innovation, since entrepreneurs are often the first to come up with new products, services, and technologies.

For instance, tech startups like Uber and Airbnb have shaken up traditional industries by coming up with new business models and taking on the big players. In the same way, companies like Tesla and SpaceX have pushed the limits of technology and innovation, which could change whole fields.

Social Entrepreneurship

In the past few years, people have become more interested in social entrepreneurship, which is when business principles are used to solve social or environmental problems (Mair & Marti, 2006).

Social entrepreneurship can take many forms, including non-profit organisations, social enterprises, and for-profit ventures with a social mission (Dees & Anderson, 2006). These ventures can help to address a range of social issues, from poverty and inequality to environmental sustainability.

For example, the TOMS Shoes brand has become known for its "One for One" model, in which the company donates a pair of shoes to a child in need for every pair sold. In a similar way, Warby Parker has shaken up the eyewear industry with its stylish, affordable glasses and commitment to making a difference in the world.

The Challenges of Entrepreneurship

Even though there may be benefits to being an entrepreneur, entrepreneurs also have to deal with a number of problems. These can include financial risks, regulatory barriers, and competition (Gompers & Lerner, 2001).

Also, being an entrepreneur can be difficult and stressful, and it can take a lot of time, energy, and money to do well. Because of this, entrepreneurs need to be strong and able to change when things don't go as planned.

The Role of Government and Policy

Lastly, it is important to think about what the government and policy can do to help entrepreneurs. (Storey, 2011) says that government policies and programmes can be a big help to entrepreneurs and to the growth of the economy.

For example, policies that promote access to funding, reduce regulatory barriers, and encourage innovation can help to create a supportive environment for entrepreneurship. In addition, programs that provide training and support for entrepreneurs can help to build the skills and knowledge necessary for success.

Entrepreneurship could help the economy grow, encourage new ideas, and solve social and environmental problems. However, it is important to recognise the challenges and risks associated with entrepreneurship, and to create a supportive environment that encourages and enables entrepreneurship to thrive.

The impact of entrepreneurship on society

Entrepreneurship is a key factor in economic growth and job creation, and its effects on society go far beyond money. Entrepreneurship is good for the economy, but it also helps people and the environment (Mair & Marti, 2006).

Entrepreneurship plays a crucial role in addressing social challenges and promoting sustainable development. Social entrepreneurship, in particular, has emerged as a significant force for creating social value and addressing issues such as poverty, inequality, and environmental degradation (Mair & Marti, 2006). For example, organisations like TOMS Shoes and Warby Parker have integrated social missions into their business models, such as donating shoes and eyeglasses to those in need with every purchase.

Entrepreneurship also has the potential to create positive spill over effects within a community. Entrepreneurial activity has been shown to increase innovation, productivity, and job creation within a region (Stam, 2015). Additionally, the presence of successful entrepreneurs can inspire and encourage others to pursue their own ventures, creating a culture of entrepreneurship and innovation.

However, entrepreneurship is not without its challenges and risks. Government policies and regulations can significantly impact the success of entrepreneurial ventures (Storey, 2011). Furthermore, while entrepreneurship can lead to positive outcomes, it can also result in negative social and environmental impacts if not managed responsibly (Santos & Eisenhardt, 2009).

Entrepreneurship has a big effect on society. It helps the economy grow and creates jobs, and it also helps solve social and environmental problems. It is important for policymakers, entrepreneurs, and stakeholders to work together to promote responsible and sustainable entrepreneurship that benefits society as a whole.

Corporate social responsibility

Corporate Social Responsibility (CSR) is the responsibility of businesses to act in a way that promotes positive social, environmental, and economic outcomes (Carroll, 1991). CSR can take many forms, such as charitable giving, ethical labour practices, environmental sustainability, and community involvement (Carroll, 1991).

CSR is becoming more and more important for businesses, and people expect them to act in a socially responsible way (Porter & Kramer, 2006). CSR can also lead to financial benefits for businesses, like a better reputation, loyal customers, and happy employees (Porter & Kramer, 2006).

Many businesses have embraced CSR as a core part of their operations. For example, Patagonia is a clothing company that has made environmental sustainability a key part of its business model, using recycled materials and promoting responsible manufacturing practices. Another example is Ben & Jerry's, an ice cream company that has a strong commitment to social justice and environmental sustainability, supporting causes such as climate justice and LGBTQ+ rights.

However, there are also criticisms of CSR, with some arguing that it is a form of "greenwashing" or "window-dressing" that allows companies to continue operating in ways that harm the environment and society (Grayson & Hodges, 2004). Others argue that CSR is a distraction from the core purpose of a business, which is to maximise profits (Friedman, 1970).

CSR is an important issue for businesses and stakeholders, and it can lead to both social and financial benefits. But it's also important to know the possible criticisms and limits of CSR and to make sure it's not used as a way to avoid bigger social and environmental problems.

Creating a sustainable business

Elkington (1994) says that building a sustainable business means making a company that can make money and have a small effect on the environment and society. This approach takes into account the fact that a business can't run in a vacuum and aims to create long-term value for all stakeholders.

One key aspect of creating a sustainable business is environmental sustainability. This involves reducing the company's carbon footprint and minimising waste and pollution through efficient resource use and sustainable practices (Eccles & Serafeim, 2013). For example, companies may seek to reduce energy use, source materials from sustainable sources, and use renewable energy sources such as solar or wind power.

Social sustainability is another important aspect of creating a sustainable business. This involves ensuring that the company's operations and products are socially responsible and ethical, and that the company contributes to the well-being of society as a whole (Elkington, 1994). For example, a company may prioritise fair labour practices, promote diversity and inclusion, and contribute to local communities through charitable giving or volunteer work.

Having a long-term view and being willing to invest in the future are also important for a business to be successful. This may involve investing in research and development to create innovative, sustainable products, or making strategic investments in sustainable infrastructure such as public transportation or renewable energy systems (Eccles & Serafeim, 2013).

Eccles and Serafeim (2013) say that companies that put sustainability first can save money in a number of ways, such as by lowering their operating costs, becoming more efficient, and improving their reputation and customer loyalty. For example, Unilever has made sustainability a key part of its business model, and has seen financial benefits such as increased revenue and reduced costs through sustainable practices (Eccles & Serafeim, 2013).

To make a business sustainable, you have to minimise its effects on the environment and on people's lives while also giving stakeholders long-term value. This approach can help people and the environment, and it can also help people's wallets.

xi. Entrepreneurship and the Future - Sustainable Development Goals

Introduction to Sustainable Development Goals

The United Nations set up 17 global goals called the Sustainable Development Goals (SDGs) in 2015 as part of the 2030 Agenda for Sustainable Development (United Nations, 2015). The SDGs try to solve some of the most important problems in the world, like poverty, inequality, climate change, and damage to the environment.

The SDGs are based on how well the Millennium Development Goals (MDGs) worked. The MDGs were set up in 2000 and aimed to reduce poverty and improve health and education in developing countries (United Nations, 2015). The SDGs, on the other hand, are more thorough and cover a wider range of issues, such as economic growth, social inclusion, and the sustainability of the environment.

The 17 SDGs are interconnected and cover a range of areas, including:

- No Poverty
- Zero Hunger
- Good Health and Well-being
- Quality Education
- Gender Equality
- Clean Water and Sanitation
- Affordable and Clean Energy
- Decent Work and Economic Growth
- Industry, Innovation and Infrastructure
- Reduced Inequalities
- Sustainable Cities and Communities
- Responsible Consumption and Production
- Climate Action
- Life Below Water
- Life on Land
- Peace, Justice and Strong Institutions
- Partnerships for the Goals

The SDGs are meant to apply to all countries, no matter how far along in development they are. They are meant to be a road map for sustainable development that can help governments, businesses, and civil society decide on policies, decide how to spend money, and take other actions.

The SDGs represent a comprehensive and ambitious global agenda for sustainable development. They address a wide range of social, economic, and environmental issues and provide a roadmap for governments, businesses, and civil society to work towards a more sustainable future.

Definition and background

The United Nations General Assembly adopted the Sustainable Development Goals (SDGs) in 2015 as part of the 2030 Agenda for Sustainable Development (United Nations, 2015). The SDGs are a set of 17 global goals. The SDGs are meant to be a call to action for everyone to end poverty, protect the planet, and make sure that by 2030, everyone has peace and prosperity.

The MDGs (Millennium Development Goals) were set up in 2000 to deal with poverty, hunger, disease, and other social and economic problems in developing countries (United Nations Development Programme, n.d.). The SDGs were made as a follow-up to the MDGs. While the MDGs were successful in some areas, they had limitations in terms of their scope and coverage.

The SDGs are more comprehensive and address a broader range of issues than the MDGs. They include economic growth, social inclusion, and environmental sustainability, among other areas. The SDGs are designed to be a universal agenda and apply to all countries, regardless of their level of development.

The SDGs were made through a process that included and encouraged participation from governments, civil society, and other important groups (United Nations, 2015). During the process of making the SDGs, people from many different groups, such as academia, civil society organisations, and the private sector, gave their input.

The SDGs are a comprehensive and ambitious global agenda for sustainable development. They build upon the successes of the MDGs and address a broader range of social, economic, and environmental challenges. The SDGs were developed through a participatory and inclusive process that involved input from a wide range of stakeholders.

Purpose of SDGs

The purpose of the Sustainable Development Goals (SDGs) is to provide a framework for global action to end poverty, protect the planet, and ensure that all people can live in peace and prosperity by 2030 (United Nations, 2015). The SDGs are meant to be a global plan that all countries, no matter how developed they are, can follow.

The SDGs are designed to be interconnected and address a wide range of issues, including poverty, hunger, health, education, gender equality, clean water and sanitation, affordable and clean energy, decent work and economic growth, industry, innovation and infrastructure, reduced inequalities, sustainable cities and communities, responsible consumption and production, climate action, life below water, life on land, peace, justice and strong institutions, and partnerships for the goals (United Nations, 2015). The SDGs aim to promote sustainable development in all these areas by balancing economic, social, and environmental priorities.

The SDGs are also meant to change the world by putting it on a path that is more sustainable and fair. For this change to happen, governments, civil society, the private sector, and individuals will all need to work together (United Nations, 2015).

The SDGs are meant to give everyone a shared plan for sustainable development that can guide actions around the world for the next 10 years and beyond. The SDGs aim to address the most pressing challenges facing the world today and create a better future for all.

Overview of the 17 SDGs

Brief explanation of each goal

1. No Poverty: This goal aims to end all kinds of poverty, including extreme poverty and multidimensional poverty, by putting in place social protection systems, making it easier for people to get basic services, and giving the poor and vulnerable ways to make a living that are sustainable.

2. Zero Hunger: This goal aims to end hunger and malnutrition by increasing agricultural productivity, promoting sustainable agriculture, improving access to healthy food, and strengthening food systems.

3. Good Health and Well-being: This goal aims to ensure universal access to quality health care services, including prevention, treatment, and promotion of mental health, and reducing the burden of communicable and non-communicable diseases.

4. Quality Education: This goal seeks to ensure that all children, youth, and adults have access to inclusive and equitable education, including early childhood development, primary, secondary, and tertiary education, and vocational training.

5. Gender Equality: This goal aims to achieve equality between men and women and give all women and girls more power. It does this by getting rid of all forms of discrimination and violence against women and girls, making sure that everyone has the same access to education and jobs, and encouraging women to lead and take part.

6. Clean Water and Sanitation: This goal seeks to ensure universal access to safe drinking water, sanitation, and hygiene, and improving water quality and wastewater management.

7. Affordable and Clean Energy: This goal aims to increase the amount of renewable energy in the world's energy mix, improve energy efficiency, and make sure that everyone has access to modern, affordable, and reliable energy services.

8. Decent Work and Economic Growth: This goal aims to promote sustained and inclusive economic growth, full and productive employment, and decent work for everyone. This includes reducing informal work and addressing labour rights and working conditions.

9. Industry, Innovation and Infrastructure: This goal aims to promote sustainable and inclusive industrialisation, enhance

innovation capacity and technological adoption, and improve access to reliable and sustainable infrastructure.

10. Reduced Inequalities: This goal aims to reduce inequality within and between countries. It does this by reducing income inequality, addressing social exclusion and discrimination, and promoting policies that help the most vulnerable people.

11. Sustainable Cities and Communities: This goal aims to make cities and human settlements inclusive, safe, resilient, and sustainable, including promoting affordable and sustainable housing, improving urban planning and management, and enhancing urban resilience to disasters and climate change.

12. Responsible Consumption and Production: This goal aims to encourage sustainable ways of consuming and making things, such as reducing waste, making better use of resources, and promoting sustainable production and consumption practices.

13. Climate Action: This goal aims to take urgent action to combat climate change and its impacts, including reducing greenhouse gas emissions, increasing adaptation and resilience to climate change, and promoting low-carbon and climate-resilient development.

14. Life Below Water: This goal aims to protect the oceans, seas, and marine resources and use them in a way that doesn't harm them in the long run. This includes reducing marine pollution, protecting marine biodiversity, and promoting sustainable fisheries.

15. Life On Land: This goal aims to protect, restore, and promote the sustainable use of terrestrial ecosystems, including forests, deserts, and mountains, as well as combatting desertification, halting and reversing land degradation, and halting biodiversity loss.

16. Peace, Justice and Strong Institutions: This goal seeks to promote peaceful and inclusive societies, provide access to justice for all, and build effective, accountable, and inclusive institutions at all levels, including reducing violence, corruption, and promoting human rights.

17. Partnerships for the Goals: This goal aims to strengthen the means of implementation and revitalise the global partnership for sustainable development. This includes promoting partnerships between governments, civil society, the private sector, and individuals to reach the SDGs.

To reach these goals, everyone, including governments, civil society organisations, the private sector, and individuals, needs to work together and do their part. Each goal is interconnected and must be approached in

Importance of each goal

The Sustainable Development Goals (SDGs) are an attempt to solve some of the most important economic, social, and environmental problems in the world. Each goal represents a significant milestone towards achieving sustainable development, and has its unique importance in creating a better future for all.

Goal 1: No Poverty – Eradicating extreme poverty is essential for creating a fairer and more equitable society. By reducing poverty, access to basic resources like food, clean water, and healthcare will be improved. According to the World Bank, the proportion of people living in extreme poverty globally fell from 36% in 1990 to 10% in 2015, indicating significant progress towards this goal.

Goal 2: Zero Hunger – Ensuring access to adequate food and improving nutrition is essential for a healthy society. The Food and Agriculture Organisation (FAO) reported that in 2019, almost 690 million people were undernourished, with the COVID-19 pandemic expected to further worsen the situation. Achieving zero hunger would ensure that everyone has access to sufficient and nutritious food.

Goal 3: Good Health and Well-being – This goal aims to improve healthcare access and promote healthy lifestyles, leading to better health outcomes for all. In 2020, the COVID-19 pandemic highlighted the importance of strong healthcare systems in responding to crises. According to the World Health Organisation (WHO), investing in good health and well-being can result in significant economic benefits, with an estimated return of US $1.50 for every US $1 invested.

Goal 4: Quality Education – Education is vital for personal and professional development, leading to more opportunities and better livelihoods. Quality education can also promote equality, tolerance, and social cohesion. According to UNESCO, more than 91% of children worldwide were enrolled in primary education in 2018, indicating progress towards this goal. However, there is still work to be done to ensure access to quality education for all.

Goal 5: Gender Equality – Gender equality is not only a fundamental human right but is also essential for sustainable economic growth.

According to the World Economic Forum, the global gender gap can cost the world economy an estimated US $160 trillion in lost productivity over the next 50 years. Achieving gender equality can improve workforce participation and productivity, leading to economic growth and development.

Goal 6: Clean Water and Sanitation – Access to clean water and sanitation is essential for promoting health and reducing the spread of diseases. According to the United Nations (UN), over 2 billion people lack access to safe drinking water, and over 4 billion people lack access to adequate sanitation facilities. Achieving this goal can improve health outcomes and economic productivity.

Goal 7: Affordable and Clean Energy – Access to affordable and clean energy is essential for sustainable development. The International Energy Agency (IEA) reported that in 2018, an estimated 840 million people globally had no access to electricity, with the majority of them in sub-Saharan Africa. Achieving this goal can promote economic growth, reduce poverty, and improve environmental sustainability.

Goal 8: Decent Work and Economic Growth – Creating decent work opportunities and promoting sustainable economic growth are essential for reducing poverty and inequality. The UN reports that global unemployment rates reached 6.5% in 2020, with the COVID-19 pandemic causing widespread job losses. Achieving this goal can improve living standards and promote economic development.

Goal 9: Industry, Innovation and Infrastructure – This goal aims to promote sustainable industrialisation, foster innovation, and develop resilient infrastructure. Investment in infrastructure can create jobs, promote economic growth, and improve access to essential services. For example, the UN reported that in 2019, over 1 billion people worldwide lacked access to electricity, with infrastructure development needed to bridge this gap. Sustainable industrialisation can also help to promote technological advancement and improve productivity, leading to economic growth.

Goal 10: Reduced Inequalities – Reducing inequalities is crucial for creating a fairer and more equitable society. The UN reports that income inequality has increased in many countries, with the richest 1% of the global population owning more than twice as much wealth as the poorest 50%. Achieving this goal can improve social cohesion and promote economic development.

Goal 11: Sustainable Cities and Communities – This goal aims to create more sustainable, resilient, and inclusive cities and communities. According to the UN, more than half of the global population lives in urban areas, with this number expected to increase to 68% by 2050. Achieving this goal can promote economic development, reduce environmental impact, and improve quality of life for urban residents.

Goal 12: Responsible Consumption and Production – This goal focuses on promoting sustainable consumption and production patterns to reduce waste, conserve resources, and reduce environmental impact. According to the UN, global material use has tripled since 1970, with an estimated 92.8 billion tonnes of materials consumed in 2017. Achieving this goal can improve environmental sustainability, reduce waste, and promote economic development.

Goal 13: Climate Action – Climate change poses a significant threat to global development, with its effects felt across all SDGs. Achieving this goal involves taking action to reduce greenhouse gas emissions, increase resilience to the impacts of climate change, and promote sustainable development. According to the Intergovernmental Panel on Climate Change (IPCC), limiting global warming to 1.5°C will require transformative change across all sectors of the economy.

Goal 14: Life Below Water – This goal aims to promote the conservation and sustainable use of oceans, seas, and marine resources. According to the UN, overfishing, pollution, and climate change have all contributed to the degradation of marine ecosystems. Achieving this goal can promote economic development, support food security, and conserve marine biodiversity.

Goal 15: Life on Land – This goal focuses on promoting the conservation and sustainable use of terrestrial ecosystems, forests, and biodiversity. According to the UN, deforestation, desertification, and land degradation continue to pose significant challenges to sustainable development. Achieving this goal can promote economic development, support food security, and conserve terrestrial biodiversity.

Goal 16: Peace, Justice, and Strong Institutions – This goal aims to promote peaceful and inclusive societies, provide access to justice for all, and build effective, accountable, and inclusive institutions. According to the UN, conflict, violence, and human rights abuses continue to threaten global development. Achieving this goal can promote social cohesion, economic development, and political stability.

Goal 17: Partnerships for the Goals – This goal emphasises the importance of partnerships and collaboration in achieving the SDGs. Achieving the SDGs will require the collective effort of governments, civil society, the private sector, and other stakeholders. Partnerships can help to leverage resources, share knowledge and expertise, and promote cooperation towards common goals.

The SDGs represent a roadmap towards a sustainable and equitable future for all. Achieving these goals will require significant effort and cooperation from all sectors of society. However, the benefits of achieving the SDGs are clear, with improved social, economic, and environmental outcomes for people and the planet.

SDGs and Entrepreneurship

The Sustainable Development Goals (SDGs) and entrepreneurship go hand in hand because entrepreneurs can help achieve the SDGs by boosting economic growth, encouraging innovation, and creating jobs. Entrepreneurs are in a unique position to find and solve social problems and create business models that are sustainable and aligned with the SDGs.

For example, companies like Patagonia and Allbirds have made products that are sustainable and good for the environment. These products are in line with the SDGs on responsible production and consumption. These companies' business models are based on sustainability, and they have done well financially while also working to protect the environment.

Entrepreneurship can also help reach the SDGs for gender equality, since it can help the economy grow and give women more power. For example, a study by the International Finance Corporation (IFC) found that businesses run by women in emerging markets can help the economy grow, create jobs, and reduce poverty.

Also, entrepreneurship can help develop developing countries in a sustainable way by creating jobs and reducing poverty. For example, microfinance institutions help people with low incomes start and grow their own businesses by giving them loans. These businesses can create jobs and promote economic growth, contributing to the SDGs on decent work and economic growth.

Entrepreneurship is a key part of reaching the SDGs because it drives economic growth, encourages new ideas, and creates jobs. Entrepreneurs can find problems in society and make business models that are sustainable and fit with the SDGs. Because of this, entrepreneurs have the potential to make big changes towards a more sustainable and fair future for everyone.

How entrepreneurship can contribute to achieving SDGs

Entrepreneurship is a key part of reaching the Sustainable Development Goals (SDGs) because it can lead to new ways of dealing with difficult social, environmental, and economic problems. Entrepreneurs can create sustainable businesses that have a positive effect on communities and help reach the SDGs by finding new opportunities and using resources well.

One way entrepreneurship can contribute to achieving the SDGs is by promoting economic growth and job creation. Small and medium-sized businesses (SMEs) are the backbone of many economies, and they can be a great way to find work and make money. The International Finance Corporation (IFC) says that SMEs make up about 90% of businesses around the world and employ more than 50% of the world's workers. By supporting the growth and development of SMEs, entrepreneurship can contribute to SDG 8 - Decent Work and Economic Growth.

Entrepreneurship can also help reach the SDGs by coming up with new ways to deal with social and environmental problems. For example, a startup called Bempu Health developed a low-cost neonatal temperature monitoring device that has helped reduce infant mortality rates in India. The device helps detect hypothermia in new-borns, a leading cause of death in developing countries. By developing innovative solutions that address social and environmental challenges, entrepreneurship can contribute to several SDGs, including SDG 1 - No Poverty, SDG 2 - Zero Hunger, SDG 3 - Good Health and Well-being, and SDG 6 - Clean Water and Sanitation.

Entrepreneurship can also promote sustainable practices and resource efficiency, contributing to SDG 9 - Industry, Innovation and Infrastructure, and SDG 12 - Responsible Consumption and Production. For example, the Swedish startup, Oatly, developed a range of plant-based milk alternatives that require less water and land to produce than traditional dairy products. By promoting sustainable practices, entrepreneurship can help reduce negative impacts on the environment and contribute to more sustainable production and consumption patterns.

Overall, entrepreneurship has the potential to make a big difference in reaching the SDGs by boosting economic growth, solving social and environmental problems, and promoting sustainable practices. Policymakers and organisations can use the power of entrepreneurship to help reach the SDGs by creating an environment that supports innovation and sustainable business practices.

Examples of successful businesses contributing to SDGs

There are numerous examples of successful businesses that have contributed to achieving the SDGs. One such example is the clothing company Patagonia, which has made sustainability and environmental responsibility central to its business model. The company has committed to using recycled materials in its products and reducing its carbon footprint, as well as donating 1% of its annual sales to environmental causes through its "1% for the Planet" program.

Another example is the Danish renewable energy company Ørsted, which has transformed itself from a fossil fuel-based energy company to a leader in renewable energy. The company has set ambitious targets for reducing its carbon footprint and increasing its renewable energy capacity, and has been recognised for its commitment to sustainable practices by being named the world's most sustainable company in 2020 by Corporate Knights.

In the financial sector, the Dutch bank Triodos Bank has focused on using its investments to promote sustainable development, with a particular focus on renewable energy and social enterprise. The bank's lending practises have helped a lot of sustainable energy projects and social enterprises grow. They have also helped more people get access to credit and helped their communities grow.

More Examples:

➤ Tesla - Tesla is an electric vehicle and clean energy company that is working towards a sustainable future. Their mission is to accelerate the transition to sustainable energy. Tesla's products, such as electric cars and solar panels, are helping to reduce greenhouse gas emissions and combat climate change.

➤ Grameen Bank - Grameen Bank is a microfinance institution founded by Muhammad Yunus, which provides small loans to impoverished individuals to start their own businesses. By empowering individuals to become entrepreneurs and start their own businesses, Grameen Bank is contributing to SDG

1 (No Poverty) and SDG 8 (Decent Work and Economic Growth).

➢ Ecocem - Ecocem is an Irish cement company that produces low-carbon cement, which reduces the carbon footprint of the construction industry. Their product has helped to reduce CO_2 emissions from cement production by up to 70%.

➢ Fairphone - Fairphone is a Dutch smartphone company that is committed to ethical and sustainable manufacturing practices. They aim to create a more sustainable electronics industry by using responsibly sourced materials and reducing waste. Fairphone's products are helping to promote responsible consumption and production (SDG 12).

➢ Unilever - The company has set out to achieve several SDGs, including SDG 3 (Good Health and Well-being), SDG 5 (Gender Equality), SDG 6 (Clean Water and Sanitation), and SDG 8 (Decent Work and Economic Growth). Unilever's Sustainable Living Plan outlines its strategy to improve the health and well-being of people, reduce the company's environmental footprint, and create sustainable livelihoods.

These examples show how businesses can make a big difference in achieving the SDGs while also making money and making their stakeholders' lives better. By building sustainability and social responsibility into their business models, these companies have shown that it is possible to make money and do good for society and the environment at the same time.

Challenges and Opportunities

Challenges facing the achievement of SDGs

The Sustainable Development Goals (SDGs) are a big plan for the whole world. They aim to solve some of the most important social, economic, and environmental problems that the world is facing right now. But these goals can't be reached without a lot of work from everyone involved, including governments, businesses, civil society groups, and individuals. Some of the key challenges facing the achievement of SDGs include:

> ➢ Insufficient Financing: To reach the SDGs, a lot of money needs to be invested in infrastructure, education, health care, and other key areas. However, there is a significant financing gap that needs to be addressed. According to the UN, the annual financing gap for SDGs is estimated to be between $2.5 and $3 trillion. This requires innovative financing mechanisms and increased private sector investments to bridge the gap.

➤ Lack of political will: For the SDGs to be put into place, governments need to have strong political will and commitment. But there isn't always the political will to put these goals at the top of the list, especially in countries with political or economic problems.

➤ Inadequate data and monitoring: Measuring progress towards achieving SDGs requires accurate and timely data. However, many countries lack the necessary data systems and monitoring mechanisms to track progress towards these goals.

➤ Climate change and environmental degradation: Climate change and environmental degradation pose significant challenges to achieving SDGs, particularly those related to poverty reduction, clean water and sanitation, and sustainable cities and communities. The effects of climate change, such as natural disasters and food insecurity, can also undermine progress towards achieving other SDGs.

➤ Inequality and social exclusion: Inequalities and social exclusion remain major barriers to achieving SDGs. These include inequalities in access to education, healthcare, and employment opportunities, as well as discrimination based on gender, ethnicity, and other factors.

Despite these challenges, there are many examples of successful initiatives and partnerships aimed at advancing SDGs. For instance, the UN Global Compact initiative brings together businesses, governments, and civil society organisations to advance sustainable development, and has been instrumental in promoting sustainable business practices worldwide. Another example is the "Green Deal" initiative launched by the European Union, which aims to make the EU carbon-neutral by 2050 and has already generated significant investments in renewable energy and other sustainable infrastructure.

In Ireland, the Sustainable Energy Authority of Ireland (SEAI) has been promoting the use of renewable energy and sustainable practises through different programs, such as the Better Energy Communities Scheme, which helps community-based energy efficiency projects. This initiative has helped to reduce carbon emissions and energy costs, while also creating jobs and promoting social inclusion.

Overall, addressing the challenges facing the achievement of SDGs requires a collective effort from all stakeholders, and innovative solutions that balance economic growth with environmental sustainability and social equity.

Opportunities for businesses to contribute to SDGs

Opportunities for businesses to contribute to SDGs are vast and varied, with each industry having its unique contribution to sustainable development. By aligning their business strategies with the SDGs, companies can create value for both their business and society.

One of the most significant opportunities for businesses is to adopt sustainable business practices. This includes incorporating environmental, social, and governance (ESG) factors into their operations, such as reducing greenhouse gas emissions, promoting employee well-being, and ensuring supply chain sustainability. For example, Patagonia, a clothing company, has incorporated sustainable practices into its supply chain, such as using recycled materials in their products and implementing fair labour practices in their factories.

Another chance for businesses is to come up with new products and services that solve problems related to sustainability. For example, Tesla's electric cars help reduce greenhouse gas emissions and make transportation more environmentally friendly. In a similar way, the Dutch company Fairphone has made a sustainable smartphone that is easy to repair and upgrade and is made from materials that are sourced in an ethical way.

Also, businesses can help reach the SDGs by working with other groups, like governments, NGOs, and other businesses. This can be done by taking part in public-private partnerships, giving money to charitable causes, or lobbying for change. For example, the World Wildlife Fund has teamed up with the Coca-Cola Company to promote sustainable farming practises and protect freshwater resources.

Businesses can create value for their shareholders, customers, employees, and communities by contributing to the SDGs. However, to fully leverage the opportunities presented by the SDGs, businesses must overcome various challenges, such as regulatory and policy barriers, lack of resources, and stakeholder resistance.

Overall, businesses have a big part to play in meeting the SDGs and making sure everyone has a good future. Businesses can contribute to sustainable development and make money for themselves at the same time by using green practices, coming up with new ideas, and working with other stakeholders.

Best Practices for SDGs

The best way to reach the SDGs is through a multi-stakeholder approach that includes governments, businesses, civil society, and people. To reach the SDGs, people and organisations must work together and form partnerships. No one organisation or person can solve the world's complex problems on their own. Some of the best ways to reach the SDGs are to include them in core business strategies, set goals that are both big and measurable, use sustainable practises all along the value chain, and report openly on progress towards reaching the SDGs.

One example of a company that has integrated the SDGs into its core business strategy is Unilever. For example, Unilever wants to use 100% renewable energy in its operations by 2030 and cut its environmental footprint in half by 2030. The company has also launched a sustainable living plan, which focuses on creating sustainable products, reducing waste, and improving the livelihoods of workers in its supply chain.

Danone is another example. They want to be carbon neutral by 2050 and have put in place sustainable practises all along their value chain. For instance, the company has developed a regenerative agriculture program, which focuses on soil health and biodiversity, and has launched a packaging innovation program to reduce waste.

Engaging with stakeholders, such as customers, employees, suppliers, and communities, is also a good way to reach the SDGs. One example is Patagonia, which has a programme called "Worn Wear" that engages customers and encourages them to fix and reuse their products instead of buying new ones. The company has also engaged with employees through its commitment to fair labour practices and has partnered with communities to protect public lands and advocate for environmental conservation.

Transparency and reporting on progress towards achieving the SDGs is also critical. One example is Coca-Cola, which has published an annual sustainability report since 2007, detailing its progress towards achieving sustainability goals, including reducing water usage and greenhouse gas emissions. The company has also engaged with stakeholders through its "World Without Waste" initiative, which aims to collect and recycle a bottle or can for each one it sells by 2030.

The best way to reach the SDGs is to take a comprehensive approach that includes integrating the SDGs into core business strategies, putting in place sustainable practises all along the value chain, involving stakeholders, and reporting on progress towards reaching the SDGs in a clear way.

Examples of companies successfully contributing to SDGs

IKEA is a multinational furniture retailer that has integrated SDGs into its business strategy. The company's sustainability strategy, People & Planet Positive, focuses on three main areas: sourcing sustainable materials, reducing energy and resource use, and promoting social sustainability. IKEA has made a commitment to source 100% renewable energy by 2025 and to make its products from renewable and recycled materials.

One example of how IKEA has contributed to SDGs is through its "Better Cotton" initiative. The company has partnered with the Better Cotton Initiative (BCI) to promote the sustainable production of cotton. Through this initiative, IKEA has supported the training of over 2,000 farmers in India and Pakistan in sustainable cotton farming practices. This has helped to reduce the environmental impact of cotton production and improve the livelihoods of cotton farmers.

More Examples:

➢ Unilever - Unilever is a British-Dutch consumer goods company that has made sustainability a core part of its business strategy. Its Sustainable Living Plan sets out ambitious targets, including sourcing 100% of its agricultural raw materials sustainably, halving the environmental footprint of its products, and improving the health and well-being of over 1 billion people by 2020. Unilever has been recognised as a leader in sustainability, ranking first in the 2018 Dow Jones Sustainability Index for the food and beverage sector.

➢ Patagonia - Patagonia is an American clothing company that has become well known for its commitment to environmental and social sustainability. The company has implemented a number of initiatives, including reducing the environmental impact of its supply chain, investing in renewable energy, and supporting grassroots environmental activism. In 2017, Patagonia donated 100% of its Black Friday sales to grassroots environmental organisations, raising $10 million.

➢ Danone - Danone is a French multinational food products company that has made sustainability a core part of its business strategy. Its "One Planet, One Health" initiative sets out ambitious targets, including achieving carbon neutrality by 2050 and regenerating soils and landscapes. Danone has also launched a number of innovative products, including plant-based yogurts and probiotics, that promote health and sustainability.

> Tesla - Tesla is an American electric vehicle and clean energy company that has become a leader in sustainable transportation. Its products, including electric cars, solar panels, and energy storage systems, are designed to reduce dependence on fossil fuels and promote the transition to a low-carbon economy. Tesla has been recognised as a leader in sustainability, ranking first in the 2020 Carbon Clean 200 list of clean energy companies.

> ESB - ESB is an Irish state-owned electricity company that has made sustainability a core part of its business strategy. Its "Brighter Future" strategy sets out ambitious targets, including reducing its carbon emissions by 50% by 2030 and achieving net-zero emissions by 2050. ESB has also launched a number of innovative products, including electric vehicle charging solutions and energy management systems, that promote sustainability.

> Novozymes is a Danish biotech company that focuses on making sustainable solutions for many industries, such as

agriculture, energy, and consumer goods. Their enzyme technology is used in many industries, from making biofuels to making clothes, and has been recognised for its potential to make these industries less harmful to the environment.

> Grameen Bank: The Bangladeshi microfinance institution was founded by Nobel Peace Prize winner Muhammad Yunus, and has been credited with lifting millions of people out of poverty. By providing small loans to individuals who do not have access to traditional banking services, Grameen Bank has enabled entrepreneurs to start businesses and improve their standard of living.

> Ecotricity is a UK-based energy company that works to support renewable energy and reduce carbon emissions. They have invested in wind and solar power projects, and also offer electric vehicle charging stations. In addition, they have committed to donating 50% of their profits to environmental and social initiatives.

These companies demonstrate that businesses can successfully contribute to SDGs while also creating value for their stakeholders. By integrating sustainability into their core business strategies and operations, these companies are setting an example for others to follow.

Strategies for businesses to achieve SDGs

Strategies for businesses to achieve SDGs involve integrating sustainability practices into their core business operations, supply chains, and product development. Some of the strategies include:

> Setting big goals: Companies can set big goals to reduce their environmental impact, like reducing greenhouse gas emissions or water use, and track their progress towards meeting these goals. For example, Danone, a multinational food and beverage company, has set a goal to become carbon neutral by 2050 and has taken steps to reduce its carbon footprint, such as investing in renewable energy sources and optimising its manufacturing processes.

> Collaboration and partnerships: Collaboration and partnerships can help businesses achieve SDGs by pooling resources and expertise to tackle complex challenges. For example, Nestle, a multinational food and beverage company, has partnered with the International Federation of Red Cross and Red Crescent Societies to provide clean water and sanitation facilities to communities affected by natural disasters.

➢ Sustainable supply chains: Businesses can make their supply chains more sustainable by getting their raw materials and finished goods from vendors who follow environmental and social standards. For example, Unilever, a multinational consumer goods company, has a sustainable sourcing policy that includes promises to reduce deforestation, promote biodiversity, and respect human rights in its supply chain.

➢ Innovation: Innovation can help businesses develop new products and services that promote sustainability and contribute to achieving SDGs. For example, Tesla, a US-based electric vehicle company, has developed innovative battery technology and charging infrastructure that supports the transition to renewable energy sources and helps reduce greenhouse gas emissions.

➢ Community engagement: Businesses can work with local communities to find out what they need and tackle social and environmental problems as a group. Coca-Cola, a multinational beverage company, has done things like help people get access to clean water and toilets and support education and business programs.

These strategies can help businesses work towards the SDGs and make the future more sustainable.

SDG Conclusion

The Sustainable Development Goals (SDGs) are a big step towards achieving sustainable development, as we have seen. Entrepreneurship is a key part of achieving the SDGs, and businesses have a responsibility to help reach them. Even though there are problems to solve, there are also ways for businesses to make a positive difference and make money.

Including the SDGs in business plans can lead to a number of benefits, such as more loyal customers, a better reputation for the brand, and better financial performance. Best practices for achieving the SDGs include incorporating sustainable practices into supply chain management, establishing partnerships with relevant stakeholders, and creating transparency around progress towards goals.

Companies that are doing a good job of contributing to the SDGs include Unilever, which has promised to get all of its agricultural raw materials in a sustainable way by 2020, and Patagonia, which has made a variety of products that are sustainable and good for the environment. IKEA has also done a lot to help reach the SDGs. For example, it has promised to use only renewable energy and cut its carbon footprint by 80% by 2030.

Overall, businesses need to understand their role in achieving the SDGs and work to make their operations more sustainable. By doing this, businesses can help make the future better for everyone while also making money.

Recap of key points

In summary, the Sustainable Development Goals (SDGs) provide a framework for businesses to contribute to global sustainable development, while also promoting economic growth and innovation. The 17 SDGs cover a wide range of economic, social, and environmental issues, and businesses can play a critical role in achieving these goals by integrating them into their operations and strategies.

To contribute to the achievement of SDGs, businesses must understand their responsibilities and opportunities, implement sustainable practices, and engage with stakeholders to promote sustainable development. This can involve adopting sustainable production and consumption practices, investing in renewable energy and clean technologies, providing decent work opportunities, and engaging with local communities to promote social inclusion and economic development.

By aligning their operations and strategies with the SDGs, businesses can not only contribute to sustainable development, but also benefit from a better brand reputation, more market opportunities, and fewer risks related to environmental and social challenges.

Overall, the SDGs give businesses a good way to contribute to global sustainable development. By using this framework, businesses can help make the future more prosperous, fair, and sustainable for everyone.

xii. Case Studies and Success Stories

Quick Case Study: Stripe Technologies

Introduction: Stripe Technologies is a fintech company that provides an online payment processing platform that enables businesses to receive and manage online payments. The company was founded in 2010 by Irish brothers Patrick and John Collison, who were only 22 and 19 years old respectively at the time. Stripe Technologies quickly gained attention and investment from prominent venture capitalists, and now has a valuation of over $95 billion, making it one of the most valuable private companies in the world. In this case study, we will examine how Stripe Technologies applied entrepreneurship theories to achieve success.

Entrepreneurship Theories Applied

Innovation Theory: Innovation is at the core of Stripe Technologies' success. The company recognised a gap in the market for an easy-to-use, customisable online payment platform and developed a solution that revolutionised the industry. Stripe Technologies' platform is highly customisable, allowing businesses to tailor it to their specific needs, which has been a major selling point for the company.

Resource-based theory: says that companies with valuable and unique resources will have an edge over their competitors. In the case of Stripe Technologies, the company's unique resource is its online payment platform, which is highly customisable, easy to use, and secure. This resource has enabled the company to gain a competitive advantage and grow rapidly.

Entrepreneurial Opportunity Theory: This theory says that entrepreneurs start businesses when they find opportunities that aren't being met and try to take advantage of them. In the case of Stripe Technologies, the opportunity was the need for a customisable, easy-to-use online payment platform. The company was able to build a very successful business because they saw this chance and took it.

Application of Theories: Stripe Technologies applied these theories in several ways to achieve success. Firstly, the company recognised the need for an online payment platform that was customisable and easy to use. By developing a platform that met this need, the company was able to differentiate itself from competitors and gain a competitive advantage.

Secondly, the company leveraged its unique resource, the payment platform, to gain market share. By providing a highly customisable and secure platform, Stripe Technologies was able to attract a wide range of businesses, from small startups to large corporations.

Patrick and John Collison, who started the business, finally saw the chance to be an entrepreneur and took it. They recognised the need for an easy-to-use online payment platform and took action to create a solution that met this need. Their willingness to take risks and think of new ways to do things have been key to the company's success.

Conclusion: Stripe Technologies is a prime example of how entrepreneurship theories can be applied to create a highly successful business. By recognising an opportunity, leveraging unique resources, and committing to innovation, the company was able to develop a highly customisable and secure online payment platform that has revolutionised the industry. Stripe Technologies' success demonstrates the importance of entrepreneurship in driving innovation and growth, and highlights the potential for young entrepreneurs to create successful businesses.

Quick Case Study: Dyson

Introduction: Dyson is a British technology company that is best known for its vacuum cleaners, air purifiers, and hand dryers. The company was founded by James Dyson in 1991, who had spent several years developing and perfecting his vacuum cleaner technology. Today, Dyson is a globally recognised brand with a presence in over 70 countries.

This case study will analyse Dyson's success from the perspective of entrepreneurship theories and how they have been applied in the company's development and growth.

Innovation and Creativity: One of the key factors that have contributed to Dyson's success is its innovative and creative approach to product development. James Dyson's initial idea for a bagless vacuum cleaner was born out of frustration with the poor performance of existing models. He spent several years perfecting the technology and developing prototypes before launching the first Dyson vacuum cleaner in 1993.

Dyson invests in research and development because it wants to be creative and open to new ideas. The company puts about £7 million a week into research and development, which has led to new products like the Airblade hand dryer and the Supersonic hair dryer.

Opportunity Recognition and Evaluation: Dyson's success is also due to its ability to find and judge opportunities. James Dyson saw a need for a more effective and efficient vacuum cleaner on the market and set out to make one. He also saw that his technology could be used to make other things, like hand dryers and air purifiers.

Market research and analysis have also played a crucial role in Dyson's success. The company has conducted extensive research into customer needs and preferences, which has informed its product development strategy. For example, the development of the Supersonic hair dryer was based on extensive research into hair styling habits and preferences.

Business Planning and Strategy: One reason for Dyson's success is that it has good business planning and strategy. Focusing on new ideas and technology has helped the company stand out from its competitors and build a strong brand image. Dyson's products are known for their high quality, durability, and performance, which has helped the company build a loyal customer base.

Dyson's expansion into new markets has also been carefully planned and executed. The company has invested in marketing and advertising to raise brand awareness in new markets, and has established partnerships with local distributors and retailers to ensure its products are readily available.

Conclusion: Dyson's success can be attributed to a number of important things, such as its commitment to creativity and innovation, its ability to find and evaluate opportunities, and its good business planning and strategy. By applying entrepreneurship theories in its development and growth, Dyson has been able to create a unique and successful brand that continues to innovate and grow.

Quick Case Study: Patagonia

Yvon Chouinard founded Patagonia, an American manufacturer of outdoor clothing and equipment, in 1973. The company is known for its environmental activism and commitment to sustainability. Patagonia's mission is to build the best products while doing the least possible harm to the environment.

Entrepreneurial Strategy: Patagonia's entrepreneurial strategy is to create high-quality products that last a long time, encourage customers to repair their clothes rather than replace them, and use environmentally friendly materials. Patagonia believes that sustainability is the key to long-term success, and that doing the right thing for the planet will ultimately benefit the bottom line.

Marketing and Sales: The way Patagonia markets and sells its products is based on its commitment to the environment and sustainability. The company's marketing campaigns focus on environmental activism and encourage customers to join the fight for a better world. Patagonia's marketing has been so good that its name has become a synonym for protecting the environment.

Managing Growth: Patagonia has grown rapidly over the years, but the company has always remained true to its core values. The company has a unique culture that promotes environmental sustainability. This culture shows up in the people it hires and the way it does business. Patagonia has also added outdoor clothing for men, women, and children to its line of goods.

Lessons Learned: Patagonia has been successful because it cares about the environment, makes high-quality products, and has a strong brand identity. The company's focus on sustainability has resonated with customers and has helped to build a loyal customer base. Patagonia's marketing campaigns have been successful because they have tapped into a growing consumer demand for environmentally sustainable products.

Analysing Strategies and Tactics: Patagonia's success can be attributed to several key strategies and tactics. First, the company has focused on creating high-quality products that last a long time. This has helped to build a loyal customer base that values durability and longevity over cheap and disposable products. Second, Patagonia has been successful in marketing its commitment to sustainability and the environment. The company's marketing campaigns have struck a chord with consumers who are increasingly concerned about the impact of their purchases on the planet. Finally, Patagonia has been successful in managing its growth by staying true to its core values and maintaining a strong company culture.

Conclusion: The success of Patagonia shows how important entrepreneurship is and how much one company can change the world. Patagonia's commitment to sustainability and the environment has not only helped to build a successful business but has also inspired other companies to follow suit. Patagonia's success serves as a model for other companies that want to build a successful business while making a positive impact on the world.

Success Story: Ben & Jerry's

Ben & Jerry's is an ice cream company that is known all over the world and has become a symbol of a successful business. The founders, Ben Cohen and Jerry Greenfield, started the company in 1978 in Burlington, Vermont, with a $12,000 investment. Over the years, the company has grown to become a multi-billion dollar business with a global reach.

Ben & Jerry's success can be explained by how the company has used different business ideas over the years. This case study will analyse some of these theories and how they have contributed to the company's success.

The social responsibility theory is one of the most important business ideas that Ben & Jerry's has used. The company has always cared about social and environmental issues, and this has always been a part of how it does business. For example, in 1985, the company started the Ben & Jerry's Foundation, which gives money to local groups that work for social justice and the environment. Also, the company has always made sure to get its ingredients from fair trade suppliers and to only use natural and organic ingredients.

Ben & Jerry's has also successfully applied the resource-based theory of entrepreneurship. The company has focused on building and leveraging its unique resources and capabilities to gain a competitive advantage. One of these resources is the brand's reputation for high-quality, environmentally conscious products. The company has also leveraged its distribution network, which includes its own branded stores, online channels, and partnerships with supermarkets and retailers.

Another theory that Ben & Jerry's has successfully applied is the opportunity recognition theory. The company has been able to identify and capitalise on various opportunities over the years, such as introducing new flavours and product lines, expanding its distribution network, and entering new markets. The company has also been able to recognise the potential of social media and digital marketing, and has used these channels to connect with customers and build brand loyalty.

Ben & Jerry's success can be explained by how the company has used different business ideas over the years. The company has built a highly successful brand that is known all over the world by focusing on social responsibility, using its unique resources, recognising and taking advantage of opportunities, and using innovative marketing strategies. Ben & Jerry's is a great example of how entrepreneurial theories can be used to make a business that is both successful and good for society.

Success Story: Supermac's

Pat McDonagh is an Irish entrepreneur and the founder of Supermac's, a fast-food chain with over 120 locations throughout Ireland. McDonagh first opened the doors of Supermac's in 1978 as a small fast-food outlet in County Galway, which has since grown into one of Ireland's most popular fast-food chains.

McDonagh's success with Supermac's is due to his business sense and his ability to change with the market. One of the reasons why Supermac is so successful is that it puts a lot of emphasis on using Irish ingredients that come from nearby. This has not only helped to support the local economy but has also given Supermac's a unique selling point that sets it apart from its competitors.

McDonagh has also taken advantage of how popular Irish culture and traditions are by using them in Supermac's branding and marketing campaigns. For example, Supermac's has sponsored local GAA teams and has even created a GAA-themed burger, which has helped to create a strong sense of community among its customers.

Furthermore, McDonagh has also shown an ability to innovate and diversify his business. In 2014, McDonagh acquired the SÓ Hotel Group, which has since grown into a successful hotel chain in its own right. This move allowed McDonagh to diversify his business portfolio and tap into the growing tourism industry in Ireland.

Overall, Pat McDonagh is one of Ireland's most successful business owners because of his success with Supermac's and his ability to change with the market and come up with new ideas for his business.

Success Story: The Body Shop

The Body Shop, a global beauty and personal care brand that has become synonymous with sustainability and ethical practices.

The Body Shop was started by Anita Roddick in the UK in 1976. Its goal was to sell beauty products that were inspired by nature and were ethically and sustainably made. Over the years, the company has grown to become a global brand, with a presence in over 70 countries.

The social responsibility theory is one of the most important business ideas that The Body Shop has used. The company has always cared about social and environmental issues, and this has always been a part of how it does business. For example, the company has been against animal testing and has advocated for animal rights for decades. The Body Shop also sources its ingredients ethically and sustainably, and has a program called "Community Fair Trade" that works with over 25,000 small-scale farmers and artisans in marginalised communities around the world.

The Body Shop has also successfully applied the resource-based theory of entrepreneurship. The company has focused on building and leveraging its unique resources and capabilities to gain a competitive advantage. One of these resources is the brand's reputation for high-quality, ethical, and sustainable products. The company has also leveraged its distribution network, which includes its own branded stores, online channels, and partnerships with retailers.

Another theory that The Body Shop has successfully applied is the opportunity recognition theory. The company has been able to identify and capitalise on various opportunities over the years, such as introducing new product lines, expanding its distribution network, and entering new markets. The company has also been able to recognise the potential of digital marketing, and has used these channels to connect with customers and build brand loyalty.

The Body Shop's success can be explained by how it has used different business theories over the years. The company has built a highly successful brand that is known all over the world by focusing on social responsibility, using its unique resources, recognising and taking advantage of opportunities, and using innovative marketing strategies. The Body Shop is a great example of how entrepreneurial theories can be used to make a business that is both successful and good for society.

Other Examples of successful entrepreneurs

Successful entrepreneurs are individuals who have turned their ideas into profitable ventures. Their stories inspire others to pursue their dreams and turn them into reality. Here are some examples of successful entrepreneurs:

> ➢ Sara Blakely - Founder of Spanx:

Sara Blakely started Spanx in 2000, with a mission to create comfortable and flattering undergarments for women. Sara Blakely is not only the founder of Spanx, but also a successful entrepreneur and philanthropist. Before starting Spanx, Blakely worked for Danka, a company that sold office equipment. However, she was not satisfied with her job and decided to start her own business. Blakely had the idea for Spanx after cutting off the feet of her pantyhose to wear under white pants. She recognised a gap in the market for comfortable and flattering undergarments for women, and decided to create her own solution.

Blakely started Spanx with just $5,000 of her own savings and began selling her products out of her own apartment. She faced many rejections from potential investors and retailers, but continued to persevere. Her big break came when Oprah Winfrey named Spanx one of her favourite things in 2000, and sales skyrocketed. Today, Spanx is a multi-million dollar company with products sold in over 50 countries.

> ➤ Elon Musk - Founder of Tesla and SpaceX:

Elon Musk is an entrepreneur who was born in South Africa. He has started several successful businesses, such as Tesla and SpaceX. Musk's vision for sustainable energy and space exploration has revolutionised these industries. Tesla produces electric cars that have become increasingly popular due to their eco-friendly nature and innovative design. SpaceX designs and launches rockets with the goal of making space travel accessible to more people.

Musk has a reputation for being a risk-taker and a visionary, which has helped him succeed in his ventures. However, he has also faced many challenges and setbacks along the way. For example, Tesla faced financial difficulties in its early years and Musk had to invest a significant amount of his own money to keep the company afloat. Despite these challenges, Musk continues to push the boundaries of what is possible and inspire others to do the same.

➢ Jan Koum - Co-founder of WhatsApp:

Jan Koum is a Ukrainian-born entrepreneur who co-founded WhatsApp in 2009 with Brian Acton. The app was designed to provide a simple and affordable messaging solution for smartphones. WhatsApp quickly became one of the most popular messaging apps in the world, with over 2 billion users.

Koum's success story is a testament to the power of simplicity and user experience. He recognised that many messaging apps were too complex and difficult to use, and decided to create a solution that was easy and accessible for everyone. Koum's focus on simplicity and user experience has helped WhatsApp become one of the most widely used apps in the world.

.

> Oprah Winfrey - Media mogul:

Oprah Winfrey is a media mogul who started her career as a talk show host. She went on to launch her own production company and network, which produces some of the most popular shows on television. Winfrey's success story shows the power of perseverance and hard work.

In the beginning of her career, Winfrey had to deal with a lot of problems and setbacks, like being fired from her job as a TV news anchor. However, she continued to work hard and eventually landed her own talk show, which became a huge success. Today, Winfrey is one of the most successful and influential media personalities in the world.

> Brian Chesky - Co-founder of Airbnb:

Brian Chesky is a designer and entrepreneur who co-founded Airbnb in 2008 with Joe Gebbia and Nathan Blecharczyk. The company provides a platform for people to rent out their homes and other properties to travellers. Today, Airbnb is a billion-dollar company with listings in over 220 countries.

Chesky's success story is a testament to the power of innovation and thinking outside the box. He recognised a gap in the market for affordable and authentic travel experiences, and decided to create a solution that would allow people to experience different cultures in a more personal way. Chesky has also faced challenges along the way, including regulatory issues and backlash from the hotel industry. However, he continues to innovate and expand Airbnb's offerings to meet the changing needs of travellers.

These successful business owners have not only built businesses that do well, but they have also given back to society in different ways. Their stories can encourage people who want to start their own businesses to follow their dreams and build successful businesses that help society.

Lessons learned from successful entrepreneurs.

Lessons learned from successful entrepreneurs can provide valuable insights for aspiring entrepreneurs. One common theme among successful entrepreneurs is the importance of perseverance and resilience. Many faced numerous obstacles and setbacks on their journey, but were able to persist through determination and a willingness to learn from their failures.

Another key lesson is the importance of taking calculated risks. Successful entrepreneurs often have a willingness to step outside of their comfort zone and pursue innovative ideas, even when the odds may not be in their favour. However, it's also important to carefully assess and manage risks to avoid catastrophic failures.

Effective leadership and management skills are also crucial for success. Entrepreneurs must be able to effectively manage their time, resources, and team to achieve their goals. This includes the ability to delegate tasks, communicate effectively, and make difficult decisions when necessary.

Additionally, successful entrepreneurs prioritise customer needs and satisfaction. By listening to feedback and constantly striving to improve their products or services, they are able to create a loyal customer base and establish a strong reputation in the market.

Lastly, successful entrepreneurs know how important it is to be flexible and able to change direction when needed. Conditions on the market and what people want can change quickly, so entrepreneurs must be able to change their strategies and products quickly to stay competitive.

Many successful entrepreneurs, such as Elon Musk, Jeff Bezos, and Sara Blakely, the founder of Spanx, have shown that these lessons are true. Musk has faced many problems in his pursuit of electric cars and space travel, but he has stayed true to his vision and kept coming up with new ideas. Bezos took calculated risks when he grew Amazon's business model, which is why it is now one of the biggest and most successful companies in the world. Blakely's resilience and perseverance in building Spanx into a billion-dollar business serves as an inspiration for aspiring entrepreneurs.

Overall, the lessons learned from successful entrepreneurs can provide valuable guidance for those looking to start or grow their own businesses. Entrepreneurs can increase their chances of long-term success by putting an emphasis on perseverance, risk management, good leadership, customer satisfaction, and the ability to change.

Analysing their strategies and tactics

Entrepreneurs-to-be can learn a lot from studying the strategies and tactics used by successful entrepreneurs. For example, a study by Hatten and Ruhland (2016) found that entrepreneurs who can find and take advantage of market opportunities, have a strong business plan, and build a supportive network of partners and advisors are more likely to be successful. Another study by Sørensen and Stuart (2016) found that successful entrepreneurs often have a deep understanding of their customers and are able to effectively market and sell their products or services.

Also, it's important for entrepreneurs to be flexible and ready to change their plans when they need to. A study by Blank and Dorf (2012) found that successful entrepreneurs are able to quickly iterate and test their ideas, and are not afraid to abandon strategies that are not working. Another important aspect is to develop a strong brand identity, as it can help differentiate a business from competitors and create customer loyalty (Kapferer, 2012).

Also, entrepreneurs who do well are often able to manage their money well and get money when they need it. A study by Pande and Khan (2015) found that access to financing and the ability to manage cash flow are critical factors for entrepreneurial success.

Overall, aspiring entrepreneurs can learn a lot by looking at the plans and methods of successful entrepreneurs. It shows how important it is to find market opportunities, make a good business plan, build a network of helpful people, know your customers, adapt to changes, create a strong brand identity, manage money well, and get funding.

xiii. Conclusion and Future Trends

In this book, we've seen how important entrepreneurship is for driving innovation, making jobs, and solving social and environmental problems. From developing a business idea, to raising capital, to scaling operations, entrepreneurs face a myriad of challenges and opportunities. By leveraging their creativity, resilience, and adaptability, successful entrepreneurs have the potential to create long-lasting impact both for themselves and for society.

Looking forward, the future of entrepreneurship looks promising, with the rise of new technologies, changing consumer behaviours, and increasing awareness of sustainability and social impact. We can expect to see more entrepreneurs use new technologies like artificial intelligence, blockchain, and virtual reality to make new products, services, and business models. We can also expect to see more entrepreneurs focusing on sustainable and socially responsible practices, as consumers demand more transparency and accountability from businesses.

As the world becomes more connected and globalised, entrepreneurship will continue to shape the economy and society in important ways. By embracing the opportunities and challenges of entrepreneurship, we can pave the way for a more innovative, inclusive, and sustainable future.

Review of key concepts

In this book, we've looked at many different aspects of entrepreneurship, starting with what it is, how important it is, what its benefits are, and what people usually get wrong about it. We have also looked at different theories of entrepreneurship, including economic and sociological theories, and the role of innovation and creativity.

To find and evaluate opportunities, we talked about ways to find opportunities, do market research and analysis, and figure out how likely business ideas are to work. We also talked about how important it is to have a business plan, set goals and objectives, and make a business strategy if you want to be successful.

Financing your business is an important part of being an entrepreneur, and we've looked at different ways to do that, like raising money and keeping track of money. Building a strong team is also essential, and we have covered topics such as hiring the right people, motivating and managing employees, and building a positive company culture.

Marketing and sales are very important to the success of any business, and we've looked at how to make a marketing plan, figure out who your target market is, and come up with a sales strategy. We've talked about how to manage growth, grow your business, and scale operations to achieve scalability and growth.

Managing risk and uncertainty is also a part of being an entrepreneur. We've talked about how to find and handle risks, deal with uncertainty, and get ready for the unexpected. Also looked at were the effects of entrepreneurship on society, corporate social responsibility, and how to make a business that will last.

In the case studies and success stories chapter, we looked at examples of successful entrepreneurs, lessons learned from their experiences, and strategies and tactics that contributed to their success. In the last chapter, "Conclusion and Future Trends," we went over the main ideas of the book and made predictions about how entrepreneurship will change in the future.

Overall, this book provides valuable insights and practical advice for aspiring and current entrepreneurs. By applying the lessons learned from this book, entrepreneurs can increase their chances of success and contribute positively to society and the economy.

Predictions for the future of entrepreneurship

As the world continues to change and evolve, the future of entrepreneurship is bound to follow suit. Some predictions for the future of entrepreneurship include:

> Increased focus on sustainable entrepreneurship: With the Sustainable Development Goals (SDGs) gaining more attention and businesses being held more accountable for their impact on society and the environment, it is likely that the future of entrepreneurship will see more emphasis on sustainable and socially responsible practices (Schaper et al., 2014).

> Growth of technology: Technology-driven entrepreneurship is on the rise. Technology is getting better and more important in every part of our lives. As a result, it is likely that the future of entrepreneurship will see a rise in

technology-driven businesses and startups (Vrontis et al., 2020).

➤ Continued importance of innovation and creativity: Innovation and creativity will continue to be important: Innovation and creativity have always been important parts of entrepreneurship, and this is likely to stay the case in the future. Entrepreneurs who are able to think outside the box and develop unique solutions to existing problems will likely continue to be successful (Naldi et al., 2015).

➤ Increased focus on collaboration and partnerships: Focus on collaboration and partnerships will grow. In order to reach the SDGs and deal with complex global problems, businesses, governments, and non-profits will likely work together and form partnerships in the future of entrepreneurship (Pickett-Baker and Ozaki, 2008).

➤ Emphasis on entrepreneurship education: As long as entrepreneurship is a key driver of economic growth and job creation, it is likely that more emphasis will be put on entrepreneurship education and training programmes to give aspiring entrepreneurs the skills and knowledge they need to succeed (Solomon et al., 2019).

In conclusion, the future of entrepreneurship is likely to see a shift towards more sustainable and socially responsible practices, an increase in technology-driven businesses, a continued focus on innovation and creativity, more collaboration and partnerships, and a greater focus on entrepreneurship education. Entrepreneurs can continue to grow the economy and help people and the environment if they follow these trends and keep coming up with new ideas and changing how they do things.

Final thoughts and recommendations

After talking about all the different parts of entrepreneurship, it's clear that it's a key part of economic growth and development. It provides opportunities for innovation, job creation, and wealth generation, among other benefits. However, to become a successful entrepreneur, one must have a deep understanding of the different concepts that make up entrepreneurship, such as identifying and evaluating opportunities, developing a business plan and strategy, financing the venture, building a strong team, marketing and sales, managing growth and risk, and the impact of entrepreneurship on society.

Moreover, as the world continues to evolve, it is important for entrepreneurs to keep up with the latest trends and adapt to changes in the business environment. Some trends that are likely to shape the future of entrepreneurship include using sustainable and socially responsible business practices, integrating technology into business operations, encouraging collaboration and partnerships, and investing in entrepreneurship education and training.

In the end, being an entrepreneur is an exciting and rewarding journey that requires commitment, hard work, and a willingness to take risks. By putting the ideas and lessons from this book to use, entrepreneurs can build businesses that do well and help the economy and society grow. Additionally, it is important to remember that entrepreneurship is not only about financial success but also about making a positive impact on society and the environment. Entrepreneurs can make the future better for everyone if they support the Sustainable Development Goals (SDGs) and run their businesses in a way that is sustainable and socially responsible.

xiv. References

(Blakely, S. (2018). Lessons from Sara Blakely: Don't be afraid to fail big. Retrieved from https://www.cnbc.com/2018/11/08/lessons-from-sara-blakely-dont-be-afraid-to-fail-big.html)

(Hossain, S., & Islam, N. (2020). Entrepreneurial success factors: An investigation through the lens of self-efficacy theory. Journal of Business Research, 113, 156-167. doi:10.1016/j.jbusres.2020.03.008)

(Pennsylvania State University. (2021). Lesson 1: Entrepreneurial Mindset: The Importance of Resilience and Perseverance. Retrieved from https://psu.instructure.com/courses/2083313/pages/lesson-1-entrepreneurial-mindset-the-importance-of-resilience-and-perseverance)

Aaker, D. A., Kumar, V., & Day, G. S. (2017). Marketing research (12th ed.). Wiley.

About Method. (2022). Method. Retrieved from https://methodhome.com/pages/about-method

Accenture. (2020). Making Global Goals Local Business – India. Retrieved from https://www.accenture.com/_acnmedia/pdf-124/accenture-making-global-goals-local-business-india.pdf

Acharya, S., & Gautam, S. (2020). Sustainability reporting practices and sustainable development goals: A content analysis. Journal of Cleaner Production, 272, 122688.

Acs, Z. J., & Stough, R. R. (2015). The determinants of entrepreneurial activity: Implications for regional policies. Handbook of Research on Entrepreneurship and Regional Development, 26-48.

Acs, Z. J., & Szerb, L. (2017). Global Entrepreneurship and Development Index 2017. Global Entrepreneurship Research Association.

Adidam, P. T., Gupta, A., & Bhatnagar, R. (2006). An empirical study of financial management practices and financial performance of small and medium enterprises. Global Journal of Finance and Economics, 3(1), 25-40.

Airbnb. (2021). About. Retrieved from https://www.airbnb.com/about/about-us.0.1287/mnsc.2014.1984

Albarran, A. B. (2019). Entrepreneurship: The art, science, and process for success (2nd ed.). Pearson.

Aldrich, H. E., & Fiol, M. (1994). Fools rush in? The institutional context of industry creation. The Academy of Management Review, 19(4), 645-670.

Aldrich, H. E., & Martinez, M. A. (2001). Many are called, but few are chosen: An evolutionary perspective for the study of entrepreneurship. Entrepreneurship Theory and Practice, 25(4), 41-56.

Allbirds. (n.d.). Sustainability. Retrieved from https://www.allbirds.com/pages/sustainability

Amabile, T. M. (1996). Creativity in context: Update to the social psychology of creativity. Westview Press.

Amorós, J. E., Bosma, N., Global Entrepreneurship Monitor, & London Business School. (2021). Global Entrepreneurship Monitor 2020/21 Global Report. London: Global Entrepreneurship Research Association.

Ansoff, H. I. (1957). Strategies for diversification. Harvard Business Review, 35(5), 113-124.

Audretsch, D. B. (2015). Everything in its place: Entrepreneurship and the strategic management of cities, regions, and states. Oxford University Press.

Bain & Company. (2019). The value of customer experience, quantified. Retrieved from https://www.bain.com/insights/the-value-of-customer-experience-quantified/

Baker, T., & Nelson, R. E. (2005). Creating something from nothing: Resource construction through entrepreneurial bricolage. Administrative Science Quarterly, 50(3), 329-366.

Barnett, C. (2013, May 14). Cleaning up: Sustainable cleaning products prove popular. Financial Times. Retrieved from https://www.ft.com/content/f36f217c-bc21-11e2-890a-00144feab7de

Barney, J. B. (1991). Firm resources and sustained competitive advantage. Journal of Management, 17(1), 99-120.

Baron, R. A. (2004). The cognitive perspective: a valuable tool for answering entrepreneurship's basic "why" questions. Journal of Business Venturing, 19(2), 221-239.

Baron, R. A., & Shane, S. A. (2008). Entrepreneurship: A Process Perspective. Cengage Learning.

Barrick, M. R., Mount, M. K., & Li, N. (2013). The theory of purposeful work behaviour: The role of personality, higher-order goals, and job characteristics. Academy of Management Review, 38(1), 132-153.

Baumol, W. J. (1990). Entrepreneurship: Productive, unproductive, and destructive. Journal of Political Economy, 98(5), 893-921.

Baumol, W. J. (2010). The microtheory of innovative entrepreneurship. Princeton University Press.

Bempu Health. (2021). Our Story. Retrieved from https://www.bempu.com/about-us

Ben & Jerry's. (n.d.). About Us. Retrieved from https://www.benjerry.com/about-us

Ben & Jerry's. (n.d.). The Ben & Jerry's Foundation. Retrieved from https://www.benjerry.com/values/how-we-do-business/the-ben-jerrys-foundation

Berger, A. N., & Udell, G. F. (2006). A more complete conceptual framework for SME finance. Journal of Banking & Finance, 30(11), 2945-2966.

Berson, Y., Oreg, S., Dvir, T., & Walter, T. (2019). Breaking the silence: How healthy conflict can improve workplace communication. Human Relations, 72(1), 54-77.

Bhide, A. (1992). Bootstrap finance: The art of start-ups. Harvard Business Review, 70(6), 109-117.

Bhide, A. (1994). Bootstrap finance: The art of start-ups. Harvard Business Review, 72(6), 109-117.

Blank, S., & Dorf, B. (2012). The startup owner's manual: The step-by-step guide for building a great company. K&S Ranch.

BMW Group. (2021). Sustainable Development Goals. Retrieved from https://www.bmwgroup.com/en/sustainability/sustainable-development-goals.html

Braunerhjelm, P., & Acs, Z. J. (2015). Entrepreneurship, institutions and economic dynamism: Lessons from a global crisis. Small Business Economics, 45(2), 203-218.

Brynjolfsson, E., & McAfee, A. (2014). The second machine age: Work, progress, and prosperity in a time of brilliant technologies. W. W. Norton & Company.

Cardon, M. S., Wincent, J., Singh, J., & Drnovsek, M. (2009). The nature and experience of entrepreneurial passion. Academy of Management Review, 34(3), 511-532.

Carroll, A. B. (1991). The pyramid of corporate social responsibility: Toward the moral management of organisational stakeholders. Business Horizons, 34(4), 39-48.

CEMEX. (2021). Sustainable Development Goals. Retrieved from https://www.cemex.com/sustainable-development-goals

Chandler, G. N., & Hanks, S. H. (1994). Market attractiveness, resource-based capabilities, venture strategies, and venture performance. Journal of Business Venturing, 9(4), 331-349.

Chandler, G. N., & Lyon, D. W. (2001). Issues of human capital and organisational capital in entrepreneurial firms. Journal of Business Venturing, 16(6), 617-634.

Chell, E. (2013). The entrepreneurial personality: A social construction. Routledge.

Chen, B. X. (2020, December 10). Airbnb's IPO filing shows a company that grew quickly, with sharp elbows. The New York Times. https://www.nytimes.com/2020/12/10/technology/airbnb-ipo-filing.html

Chen, H., & Chen, T. (2018). Venture capital financing, strategic alliances, and corporate governance: A theoretical framework. Journal of Corporate Finance, 48, 536-552.

Christensen, C. M. (1997). The innovator's dilemma: when new technologies cause great firms to fail. Harvard Business Review Press.

Coca-Cola. (2021). World Without Waste. Retrieved from https://www.coca-colacompany.com/sustainability/world-without-waste

Cohen, B. (2015). The 2008 financial crisis: An overview. Congressional Research Service.

Corporate Knights. (2020). Global 100. Retrieved from https://www.corporateknights.com/reports/2020-global-100/2020-global-100-ranking-15795684/

Danone. (2020). Danone announces commitment to become carbon neutral by 2050. Retrieved from https://www.danone.com/media/news-and-press-releases/news-releases/2020/danone-announces-commitment-to-become-carbon-neutral-by-2050.html

Danone. (2021). Our Commitments. Retrieved from https://www.danone.com/sustainability/our-commitments.html

Dees, J. G. (1998). The meaning of social entrepreneurship. Stanford Social Innovation Review, 1(1), 1-6.

Dees, J. G., & Anderson, B. B. (2006). Framing a theory of social entrepreneurship: Building on two schools of practice and thought. Research on Social Entrepreneurship, 2(1), 39-66.

Denison, D. R. (1990). Corporate culture and organizational effectiveness. John Wiley & Sons.

DiMaggio, P. J., & Powell, W. W. (1983). The iron cage revisited: Institutional isomorphism and collective rationality in organisational fields. American Sociological Review, 48(2), 147-160.

Dyson. (n.d.). About Us. Retrieved from https://www.dyson.com/about-dyson

Eccles, R. G., Ioannou, I., & Serafeim, G. (2014). The Impact of Corporate Sustainability on Organisational Processes and Performance. Management Science, 60(11), 2835–2857. doi: 1 Blakely, S. (2021). About Us - Spanx. Retrieved from https://www.spanx.com/about-us.

Ecotricity. (2021). Our Vision. Retrieved from https://www.ecotricity.co.uk/about-ecotricity/our-vision

Edmondson, A. C. (2012). Teaming: How organisations learn, innovate, and compete in the knowledge economy. John Wiley & Sons.

Emery, T. (2019). 10 Examples of Companies That Are Making Progress with the Sustainable Development Goals. Retrieved from https://www.triplepundit.com/story/2019/10-examples-companies-making-progress-sustainable-development-goals/86571

European Commission. (2021). The European Green Deal. https://ec.europa.eu/info/strategy/priorities-2019-2024/european-green-deal_en

Fairphone. (n.d.). Our Story. Retrieved from https://www.fairphone.com/en/our-story/

Feola, G. (2021). Can entrepreneurship help achieve the Sustainable Development Goals? Small Business Economics, 56(3), 899-904. doi: 10.1007/s11187-019-00238-w

Food and Agriculture Organisation. (2021). The state of food security and nutrition in the world 2020. Retrieved from http://www.fao.org/3/ca9692en/CA9692EN.pdf

Friedman, M. (1970). The social responsibility of business is to increase its profits. New York Times Magazine, 32-33.

Galgano, F. (2019, March 18). Tesla's business plan: A focus on disruption. Investopedia. https://www.investopedia.com/articles/investing/031815/teslas-business-plan-focus-disruption.asp

Gallup. (2017). State of the American workplace. Retrieved from https://www.gallup.com/workplace/238085/state-american-workplace-report-2017.aspx

Gamble, J. E., & Thompson, A. A. (2020). Essentials of strategic management: The quest for competitive advantage (6th ed.). McGraw-Hill Education.

García-Sánchez, E., Ramón-Jerónimo, M. A., Sánchez-Hernández, M. I., & González-Navarro, P. (2019). Factors affecting work-life balance and employee retention in the hotel industry. International Journal of Hospitality Management, 83, 35-44.

179

Gartner, W. B. (1988). Who is an entrepreneur? Is the wrong question. American Journal of Small Business, 12(4), 11-32.

Gaughan, P. A. (2010). Mergers, acquisitions, and corporate restructurings. John Wiley & Sons.

Germann, F., Ebbes, P., & Grewal, R. (2021). Account-Based Selling: A Framework and Research Agenda. Journal of Personal Selling & Sales Management, 41(1), 1-14.

Geron, T. (2014, March 26). Oculus VR raised $2.4 million on Kickstarter before being acquired by Facebook for $2 billion. Forbes. https://www.forbes.com/sites/tomiogeron/2014/03/26/oculus-vr-raised-2-4-million-on-kickstarter-before-being-acquired-by-facebook-for-2-billion/?sh=3db0f8dd3ea3

Gittell, J. H., Seidner, R., & Wimbush, J. (2010). A relational model of how high-performance work systems work. Organisation Science, 21(2), 490-506.

Gompers, P., & Lerner, J. (2001). The venture capital revolution. Journal of Economic Perspectives, 15(2), 145-168.

Goodall, N. (2016, June 2). How Tesla conducts market research. Forbes. https://www.forbes.com/sites/nickmorrison/2016/06/02/how-tesla-conducts-market-research/?sh=55dbd4e9240e

Goyal, M., & Kumar, R. (2020). Can entrepreneurship contribute towards achieving Sustainable Development Goals? Empirical evidence from Indian agri-business. Journal of Cleaner Production, 255, 120251. doi: 10.1016/j.jclepro.2019.120251

Graham, P. (2014). Stripe's Secret Sauce. PaulGraham.com. Retrieved from http://www.paulgraham.com/stripe.html

Grameen Bank. (2021). Who We Are. Retrieved from https://www.grameen.com/who-we-are/

Granovetter, M. (1985). Economic action and social structure: The problem of embeddedness. American Journal of Sociology, 91(3), 481-510.

Grayson, D., & Hodges, A. (2004). Corporate social opportunity!: Seven steps to make corporate social responsibility work for your business. Greenleaf Publishing.

Gross, D. (2016, December 21). How Instagram went from a $500,000 deal to a $1 billion Facebook acquisition in 18 months. Business Insider. https://www.businessinsider.com/instagrams-500000-deal-to-a-1-billion-facebook-acquisition-in-18-months-2016-12

Hardy, Q. (2016). Stripe, the $9 Billion Payments Start-Up, Thrives in the Gray Zone. The New York Times. Retrieved from https://www.nytimes.com/2016/11/27/technology/stripe-payments-start-up-thrives-in-gray-zone.html

Hatten, T. S., & Ruhland, S. K. (2016). Entrepreneurship: Successfully launching new ventures. Pearson.

Hill, C. W. L., & Jones, G. R. (2012). Strategic management: An integrated approach (10th ed.). Cengage Learning.

Hill, T., & Westbrook, R. (1997). SWOT analysis: It's time for a product recall. Long Range Planning, 30(1), 46-52.

Hisrich, R. D., Peters, M. P., & Shepherd, D. A. (2017). Entrepreneurship. McGraw-Hill Education.

Hornuf, L., & Schwienbacher, A. (2018). The Emergence of the Global Fintech Market: Economic and Technological Determinants. Journal of Business Venturing Insights, 9, 55-62.

Huddleston Jr, T. (2019, February 28). How Netflix's business strategy is crushing competitors. CNBC. https://www.cnbc.com/2019/02/28/how-netflixs-business-strategy-is-crushing-competitors.html

Humphrey, R. H., & Memili, E. (2019). The impact of the SWOT analysis: A neglected research area? Journal of Management History, 25(2), 200-212.

Hunt, V., Layton, D., & Prince, S. (2015). Diversity matters. McKinsey & Company.

IKEA. (2021). IKEA and the Sustainable Development Goals. Retrieved from https://www.ikea.com/ms/en_US/about_ikea/the_ikea_way/people_and_planet/sustainable_development_goals.html

IKEA. (2021). People & Planet Positive. https://www.ikea.com/gb/en/sustainability/people-and-planet-positive-pub8eb881f2.

Ingram, D. (2022). The Different Types of Sales Channel Strategies. Small Business - Chron.com. Retrieved from https://smallbusiness.chron.com/different-types-sales-channel-strategies-76395.html

International Energy Agency. (2021). Energy access outlook 2020. Retrieved from https://www.iea.org/reports/energy-access-outlook-2020

International Finance Corporation. (2014). She Works: Putting Gender Smart Commitments into Practice. Washington, DC: World Bank Group.

International Finance Corporation. (2021). SME Finance. Retrieved from https://www.ifc.org/wps/wcm/connect/topics_ext_content/ifc_external_corporate_site/solutions/products+and+services/sme-finance

In-text citation: (Gamble & Thompson, 2020; Starbucks Corporation, 2022)

Isenberg, D. (2010). How to start an entrepreneurial revolution. Harvard Business Review, 88(6), 40-50.

Jenkins, H. M., & Johnson, S. D. (2019). Entrepreneurial finance: a casebook. Springer.

Kapferer, J. N. (2012). The new strategic brand management: Advanced insights and strategic thinking. Kogan Page Publishers.

Kaplan, D. (2012, March 5). Dollar Shave Club: A razor-sharp example of simple marketing. Entrepreneur. https://www.entrepreneur.com/article/223494

Kelleher, L. (2019, May 4). Supermac's owner Pat McDonagh spends €3m on Dublin 4 home. Irish Examiner. Retrieved October 20, 2021, from https://www.irishexaminer.com/news/arid-30957359.html

Kim, E. (2018). How the Founders of Stripe Built a $20 Billion Business in 7 Years. CNBC. Retrieved from https://www.cnbc.com/2018/09/10/how-the-founders-of-stripe-built-a-20-billion-business-in-7-years.html

Kim, J., & Organ, D. W. (2018). Organizational celebration and recognition of employee accomplishments: A review and proposed conceptual framework. Human Resource Management Review, 28(1), 61-74.

Kim, W. C., & Mauborgne, R. (2004). Blue ocean strategy. Harvard Business Review, 82(10), 76-84.

Kim, W. C., & Mauborgne, R. (2005). Blue ocean strategy: how to create uncontested market space and make the competition irrelevant. Harvard Business Press.

Kirzner, I. M. (1973). Competition and entrepreneurship. University of Chicago Press.

Kluger, A. N., & DeNisi, A. (1996). The effects of feedback interventions on performance: A historical review, a meta-analysis, and a preliminary feedback intervention theory. Psychological Bulletin, 119(2), 254-284.

Kotler, P., & Keller, K. L. (2016). Marketing management (15th ed.). Pearson.

Kotler, P., Keller, K. L., Brady, M., Goodman, M., & Hansen, T. (2017). Marketing management (4th European ed.). Pearson.

Kotter, J. P. (2012). Accelerate! Harvard Business Review, 90(11), 44-58.

Kozlenkova, I. V., Samaha, S. A., & Palmatier, R. W. (2014). Resource-based theory in marketing. Journal of the Academy of Marketing Science, 42(1), 1-21.

Krueger, R. A., & Casey, M. A. (2015). Focus groups: A practical guide for applied research (5th ed.). Sage Publications.

Kumar, S. (2017, June 30). How Blue Apron used data to build a $2 billion meal-kit delivery business. Inc. https://www.inc.com/sangram-kumar/how-blue-apron-used-data-to-build-a-2-billion-meal-kit-delivery-business.html

Kuratko, D. F., & Hodgetts, R. M. (2017). Entrepreneurship: Theory, process, and practice. Cengage Learning.

Kuratko, D. F., & Hornsby, J. S. (2017). Entrepreneurship: Theory, process, and practice (10th ed.). Cengage Learning.

Levy, A. (2019). The Founders of Stripe Explain Why Their Radical Partnership Works. Wired. Retrieved from https://www.wired.com/story/founders-of-stripe-explain-why-radical-partnership-works/

Locke, E. A., & Latham, G. P. (2013). Goal setting theory: Setting specific goals and subgoals to improve task performance and persistence. In Handbook of principles of organisational behaviour (pp. 1-19). Wiley.

Mackey, J. (2020, June 11). A brief history of Ben & Jerry's. Investopedia. https://www.investopedia.com/articles/markets/062516/brief-history-ben-jerrys.asp

Mair, J., & Marti, I. (2006). Social entrepreneurship research: A source of explanation, prediction, and delight. Journal of World Business, 41(1), 36-44.

Marouani, M. A., & Ben Kheder, S. (2020). Entrepreneurship as a tool for achieving sustainable development goals: A review of literature. Journal of Cleaner Production, 258, 120732. doi: 10.1016/j.jclepro.2020.120732

Maurer, R. (2016). Getting the right people. Society for Human Resource Management.

Method. (2022). Methodology. Retrieved from https://methodhome.com/pages/methodology

Mollick, E. (2014). The dynamics of crowdfunding: An exploratory study. Journal of business venturing, 29(1), 1-16.

Morgeson, F. P., & Campion, M. A. (2003). Hiring the best: Managerial and organisational implications. Journal of Management, 29(4), 449-472.

Morrissey, M. (2017, March 9). How James Dyson went from failing vacuum cleaner salesman to making $3.5 billion. CNBC. Retrieved from https://www.cnbc.com/2017/03/09/how-james-dyson-went-from-failing-vacuum-cleaner-salesman-to-making-35-billion.html

Mullins, J. W., & Komisar, R. (2019). The new business road test: What entrepreneurs and executives should do before writing a business plan (5th ed.). Pearson.

Musk, E. (2021). About Tesla. Retrieved from https://www.tesla.com/about.

Naldi, L., Nordqvist, M., Sjöberg, K., & Wiklund, J. (2015). Entrepreneurial orientation, risk taking, and performance in family firms. Family Business Review, 28(1), 58-76.

Nestle. (2021). Nestle partners with International Federation of Red Cross and Red Crescent Societies to provide COVID-19 relief to communities in need. Retrieved from https://www.nestle.com/media/news/nestle-ifrc-partnership-covid-19-relief

Novozymes. (2021). About Novozymes. Retrieved from https://www.novozymes.com/about-novozymes

Oatly. (2021). Our Mission. Retrieved from https://www.oatly.com/int/about-us/mission/

O'Halloran, B. (2017, March 11). The man behind Supermac's: How Pat McDonagh became an Irish fast food giant. Independent.ie. Retrieved October 20, 2021, from https://www.independent.ie/business/irish/the-man-behind-supermacs-how-pat-mcdonagh-became-an-irish-fast-food-giant-35514984.html

Ørsted. (2021). Sustainability. Retrieved from https://orsted.com/en/sustainability

Osterwalder, A., & Pigneur, Y. (2010). Business model generation: A handbook for visionaries, game changers, and challengers. John Wiley & Sons.

Pande, P., & Khan, M. A. (2015). Entrepreneurial finance and accounting for high-tech companies. Springer.

Patagonia. (2021). Our Mission: We're in business to save our home planet. Retrieved from https://www.patagonia.com/our-mission.html

Patagonia. (2021). Worn Wear. Retrieved from https://www.patagonia.com/worn-wear.html

Patagonia. (n.d.). Environmental & Social Responsibility. Retrieved from https://www.patagonia.com/environmental-social-responsibility.html

Patagonia. (n.d.). Our Footprint. Retrieved from https://www.patagonia.com/footprint/

Patagonia. (n.d.). Our Footprint. Retrieved from https://www.patagonia.com/our-footprint/

Pickett-Baker, J., & Ozaki, R. (2008). Pro-environmental products: marketing influence on consumer purchase decision. Journal of Consumer Marketing, 25(5), 281-293.

Pinson, L., & Jinnett, J. (2019). Anatomy of a business plan: The step-by-step guide to building your business and securing your company's future. Out of Your Mind...and Into the Marketplace.

Pitts, D. W., Hicklin, A., & Hawes, J. (2018). Making inclusion an everyday reality. Harvard Business Review, 96(1), 110-117.

Porter, M. E. (1985). Competitive advantage: creating and sustaining superior performance. Simon and Schuster

Porter, M. E. (1985). Competitive advantage: creating and sustaining superior performance. Simon and Schuster.

Porter, M. E. (1996). What is strategy? Harvard Business Review, 74(6), 61-78.

Porter, M. E. (2008). The five competitive forces that shape strategy. Harvard Business Review, 86(1), 78-93.Top of Form

Porter, M. E., & Kramer, M. R. (2006). The link between competitive advantage and corporate social responsibility. Harvard Business Review, 84(12), 78-92.

Rao, L. (2020, November 20). Mailchimp's co-founders, who have never raised a dime, turned a side project into a $4.2 billion sale. CNBC. https://www.cnbc.com/2020/11/20/mailchimps-co-founders-turned-a-side-project-into-a-4point2-billion-sale.html

Ries, E. (2011). The lean startup: How today's entrepreneurs use continuous innovation to create radically successful businesses. Crown Business.

Ries, E. (2011). The lean startup: how today's entrepreneurs use continuous innovation to create radically successful businesses. Currency.

Sahlman, W. A. (1990). The structure and governance of venture-capital organisations. Journal of Financial Economics, 27(2), 473-521.

Santos, F. M., & Eisenhardt, K. M. (2009). Constructing markets and shaping boundaries: Entrepreneurial power in nascent fields. Academy of Management Journal, 52(4), 643-671.

Sarasvathy, S. D. (2001). Causation and effectuation: Toward a theoretical shift from economic inevitability to entrepreneurial contingency. Academy of Management Review, 26(2), 243-263.

Schaper, M. T., Volery, T., Weber, P. C., & Gibson, B. (2014). Entrepreneurship and small business. John Wiley & Sons.

Schoemaker, P. J. (1995). Scenario planning: A tool for strategic thinking. Sloan Management Review, 36(2), 25-40.

Schumpeter, J. A. (1934). The theory of economic development. Harvard University Press.

Schumpeter, J. A. (1934). The theory of economic development: An inquiry into profits, capital, credit, interest, and the business cycle. Harvard University Press.

Shane, S. (2000). Prior knowledge and the discovery of entrepreneurial opportunities. Organisation Science, 11(4), 448-469.

Shane, S. (2003). A general theory of entrepreneurship: The individual-opportunity nexus. Edward Elgar Publishing.

Shane, S. (2018). Entrepreneurship: A process perspective. Cengage Learning.

Shane, S. A. (2017). Entrepreneurship: A process perspective. Cengage Learning.

Shane, S., & Venkataraman, S. (2000). The promise of entrepreneurship as a field of research. Academy of Management Review, 25(1), 217-226.

Shead, S. (2019, December 30). Peloton's billion-dollar year: How a single cycling studio in New York became a connected fitness phenomenon. CNBC. https://www.cnbc.com/2019/12/30/how-peloton-became-a-4-billion-fitness-start-up.html

Slack, N., Brandon-Jones, A., & Johnston, R. (2017). Operations management (8th ed.). Pearson.

Solomon, G. T., Weaver, K. M., & Fernald, L. W. (2019). Entrepreneurship education: What we know and what we need to know. Entrepreneurship Theory and Practice, 43(2), 163-182.

Sørensen, J. B., & Stuart, T. E. (2016). Aging, obsolescence, and organisational innovation. Administrative Science Quarterly, 61(2), 359-397.

Stam, E. (2015). Entrepreneurial ecosystems and regional policy: A sympathetic critique. European Planning Studies, 23(9), 1759-1769.

Starbucks Corporation. (2022). About us. Retrieved from https://www.starbucks.com/about-us

Stevenson, H. H., & Gumpert, D. E. (1985). The heart of entrepreneurship. Harvard Business Review, 63(2), 85-94.

Stevenson, H. H., & Jarillo, J. C. (1990). A paradigm of entrepreneurship: Entrepreneurial management. Strategic Management Journal, 11(5), 17-27.

Stewart, J., & Zhao, Q. (2000). Internet accounting: A new frontier in accounting research. Journal of Accounting and Public Policy, 19(3), 209-236.

Storey, D. J. (2011). Optimism, pessimism and realism: A review of the literature on the role of government policy in supporting small and medium-sized enterprises (SMEs). International Small Business Journal, 29(3), 193-213.

Suddath, C. (2013, September 3). Soap for Society: The Method to Method's Madness. Bloomberg Businessweek. Retrieved from https://www.bloomberg.com/news/articles/2013-09-03/soap-for-society-the-method-to-method-s-madness

Supermac's. (n.d.). About Us. Retrieved October 20, 2021, from https://www.supermacs.ie/about-us

Sustainable Energy Authority of Ireland. (2021). Better Energy Communities. https://www.seai.ie/grants/home-energy-grants/better-energy-communities/

Sweney, M. (2014, January 8). Netflix's market research pays off; subscribers exceed 40m worldwide. The Guardian. https://www.theguardian.com/media/2014/jan/08/netflix-market-research-subscribers

Tesla. (2021). Tesla Battery Day. Retrieved from https://www.tesla.com/battery-day

Tesla. (n.d.). About Tesla. Retrieved from https://www.tesla.com/about

The Coca-Cola Company. (2021). Community. Retrieved from https://www.coca-colacompany.com/communities/

The University of Tennessee. (n.d.). Resource-Based Theory. Retrieved from https://leadership.memphis.edu/media/assessment-tools/Resource-Based-Theory.pdf

The World Bank. (2021). Poverty. Retrieved from https://www.worldbank.org/en/topic/poverty

Tims, M., Bakker, A. B., & Derks, D. (2013). The impact of job crafting on job demands, job resources, and well-being. Journal of Occupational Health Psychology, 18(2), 230-240.

Triodos Bank. (2021). Impact Investing. Retrieved from https://www.triodos.com/impact-investing/what-we-invest-in/

U.S. Small Business Administration. (2022). Financing Your Business. Retrieved from https://www.sba.gov/business-guide/plan-your-business/finance-your-business.

U.S. Small Business Administration. (2022). Small Business Profile. Retrieved March 30, 2023, from https://www.sba.gov/sites/default/files/advocacy/2022-Small-Business-Profiles-US.pdf

UNESCO. (2021). Primary education. Retrieved from https://en.unesco.org/themes/education-and-gender-equality/primary-education

Unilever. (2021). Our Sustainable Living Plan. Retrieved from https://www.unilever.com/sustainable-living/

Unilever. (2021). Sustainable Development Goals. Retrieved from https://www.unilever.com/sustainable-living/the-un-sustainable-development-goals/

Unilever. (2021). Sustainable sourcing. Retrieved from https://www.unilever.com/sustainable-living/reducing-environmental-impact/sustainable-sourcing/

United Nations Development Programme. (2015). Sustainable Development Goals. Retrieved from https://www.undp.org/content/undp/en/home/sustainable-development-goals.html

United Nations Development Programme. (n.d.). Millennium Development Goals. Retrieved from https://www.undp.org/content/undp/en/home/sustainable-development-goals/mdg-overview.html

United Nations Global Compact. (2017). Business and the Sustainable Development Goals: A Framework for Action. Retrieved from https://www.unglobalcompact.org/library/5461

United Nations Global Compact. (2021). About the UN Global Compact. https://www.unglobalcompact.org/about

United Nations. (2015). Transforming our world: the 2030 agenda for sustainable development. Retrieved from https://sustainabledevelopment.un.org/post2015/transformingourworld

United Nations. (2015). Transforming our world: The 2030 Agenda for Sustainable Development. Retrieved from https://www.un.org/ga/search/view_doc.asp?symbol=A/RES/70/1&Lang=E

United Nations. (2015). Transforming our world: The 2030 Agenda for Sustainable Development. Retrieved from https://www.un.org/ga/search/view_doc.asp?symbol=A/RES/70/1&Lang=ETop of Form

United Nations. (2015). Transforming our world: The 2030 agenda for sustainable development. Retrieved from https://www.un.org/sustainabledevelopment/sustainable-development-goals/

United Nations. (2019). The Sustainable Development Goals Report 2019. https://unstats.un.org/sdgs/report/2019/

United Nations. (2021). Clean water and sanitation. Retrieved from https://www.un.org/sustainabledevelopment/water-and-sanitation/

United Nations. (2021). Decent work and economic growth. Retrieved from https://www.un.org/sustainabledevelopment/economic-growth/

United Nations. (2021). Industry, innovation and infrastructure. Retrieved from https://www.un.org/sustainabledevelopment/infrastructure-industrialisation/

United Nations. (n.d.). Business and Sustainable Development. Retrieved from https://www.un.org/sustainabledevelopment/business/

Vrontis, D., Thrassou, A., & Lamprianou, I. (2020). Entrepreneurial ecosystems in transition economies: The case of Cyprus. Journal of Business Research, 112, 155-163.

Weiner, B. (2013). A theory of organisational readiness for change. Implementation Science, 8(1), 1-9.

WhatsApp. (2021). About. Retrieved from https://www.whatsapp.com/about.

Whetten, D. A. (2009). An examination of the interface between context and theory applied to the study of Chinese organisations. Management and Organisation Review, 5(1), 29-55.

Whitwam, R. (2021, March 6). The Dyson Story: How James Dyson Created His Billion Dollar Empire. Interesting Engineering. Retrieved from https://interestingengineering.com/the-dyson-story-how-james-dyson-created-his-billion-dollar-empire

Winfrey, O. (2021). Biography. Retrieved from https://www.biography.com/media-figure/oprah-winfrey.

World Economic Forum. (2021). The global gender gap report 2020. Retrieved from http://www3.weforum.org/docs/WEF_GGGR_2020.pdf

World Health Organisation. (2021). Health and economic growth. Retrieved from https://www.who.int/health_financing/documents/health_economic _growth/en/

World Wildlife Fund. (n.d.). Our Partnerships. Retrieved from https://www.worldwildlife.org/initiatives/our-partnerships

Ingram Content Group UK Ltd.
Milton Keynes UK
UKHW020353040523
421150UK00010B/59

9 781803 526867